WHAT ARE WE LIVING FOR?
PRACTICAL PHILOSOPHY
I. The Ethics

By
Chauncey D. Leake

PJD PUBLICATIONS LTD
10 Oakdale Drive, Westbury, NY 11590

Library of Congress Catalog Card No. 72-95448
International Standard Book Number. 0-9600290-2-8

WHAT ARE WE LIVING FOR?

PRACTICAL PHILOSOPHY

I. The Ethics

TO ALL who have helped me to formulate my ideas about ethical theory and practice - and they are legion, - teachers, colleagues, students, friends, and especially my wise and patient wife - this effort is dedicated, with affection and respect.

CDL

On Parnassus Heights
in San Francisco,
September 5, 1972

A Side Remark to the Reader

This book, if you go at it carefully, may change your life. If it does, I hope it will be for the better, for you, and for those with whom you come in contact.

A LISTING OF WHAT THIS BOOK CONTAINS

ABOUT THE AUTHOR

A rare combination of scientist, humanist and philosopher, Chauncey D. Leake, Litt. B., M. S., Ph.D., L. H. D., D.Sc., LL.D., is certainly well versed in life and living. This book is a testimony to it.

His many honors include a special award from the International Anesthesia Research Society; Honorary Fellowship in the American College of Dentists; Chairman, Pharmacology section of the American Medical Association; President of the American Association for the Advancement of Science; President of the Society of Experimental Biology and Medicine; President of the American Society for Pharmacology and Experimental Therapeutics; President of the History of Science Society etc.

In this series of books Dr. Leake develops a deeply philosophical discourse on the *Ethics, Logics* and *Esthetics* of a practical nature of *what we are living for.* This question is of utmost importance to everyone of us and may decide the future of our ever shrinking earth.

An editor or founding father of several journals, an author of over six hundred publications and of ten books, Chauncey Leake is senior lecturer at the University of California, San Francisco. He taught at the University of Wisconsin, the Ohio State University and was in charge, from 1942 to 1955, of the University of Texas Medical Center at Galveston. He now presents in this trilogy of books (Ethics, Logics and Esthetics) a very important modern assay of our current philosophical heritage. As he says in a side remark, studying this book may change the lives of most of us for the better.

Introductory Discussion
What It's All About,
And How It Will Be
Developed

The younger generation shows a lively inclination to stand guard at the portals of life, demanding to know by what right we of the older generation propose to determine what interests shall, and what interests shall not be pursued.

Max Otto, in
Science and the Moral Life,
1949

Ethical systems are roughly distinguishable according as they take for the cardinal ideas: (1) the character of the agent; (2) the nature of the motive; (3) the quality of the deeds and (4) the results.

Herbert Spencer, *The Data of Ethics,* 1879

Absolutism in morals is a guarantee of objectionable morals in the same way as absolutism in government is a guarantee of objectionable government.

Robert Briffault, in *Sin and Sex,* 1931

Introduction

In my opinion there is little hope for much success in this book: it is not conventional, neither in idiom, attitude nor presentation. On the other hand, I think this book offers much to intelligent people who may be impatient with the platitudinous or unintelligible jargon of current philosophy. It is an important phenomenon of our times that people generally are showing real interest in the practical philosophy of the ethics, the logics and the esthetics. This seems to me to be occurring in spite of the conventional and detailed approaches to these problems which are made by our professional philosophers. They seem usually to be talking to themselves. Most people have difficulty in understanding what they are talking about. They tend to promote an in-group language known only to the initiates. As in the case of professionals generally, they seem to resent any sort of amateur intrusion into their select groups. Thus, I can readily imagine the glee with which professional philosophers will condemn, dissect and destroy my amateurish venture into their domain.

Yet a devoted amateur of a subject may occasionally offer something worth while. I am an amateur philosopher, but the love of wisdom has been with me for over half a century. Recently I have become bold enough to presume to try to share my reflections on the ethics, the logics and the aesthetics with anyone who cares to listen. Thus, in a way, I am a teacher of philosophy, although I am neither certified nor accredited as such.

There is much danger in presuming to undertake an amateurish venture into a highly professionalized field. Ezra Pound, keen as a poet, was a failure as an operatic composer. His *Testament of François Villon,* though couched in antique French and sharp English, is a disaster musically, except for a closing motet. When given its premiere at the fine Zellerbach theater at the University of California in Berkeley, it was disappointing, in spite of an over-elaborate set design and costuming by Ariel Parkinson, our long-time friend. It prompted pertinent critique of the amateur effort. Robert Commanday, the keen music critic of the *San Francisco Chronicle,* summed it up as an attempt at "the glorification of amateurism, the eternal refuge of the superficial and the dilettante." This I will accept as pertaining to my effort here, even with the qualification of sincerity.

There can be little doubt that I am rather naive. For example, I have the unaccepted conviction that persons who are awarded the increasingly popular academic degree of Doctor of Philosophy should really know something about philosophy. They usually do not. Often they are appallingly ignorant of the great philosophical problems and of the various carefully formulated solutions which have been proposed. True, many can speak glibly of existentialism, and of Sartre, Camus, or Marcuse. This, however, tells little more than personal preoccupation with the ever receding present and gives no indication of, knowledge of, or interest in, the great practical and intensely individualized questions of which the various ethics and logics are proposed answers. Yet these questions remain for each of us, and our conscious or subconscious answers to them determine our destiny.

I thought I'd do something about getting a little philosophical interest in candidates for the degree of doctor of philosophy. I did, and the results have pleasantly surprised me.

Here I should indulge in a bit of autobiographical detail. I am in my seventies, and for more than a half century I have been interested in philosophical and especially ethical problems: not in the usual turgid and confusing jargon used by professional philosophers, but rather in the practical moral problems with which I have become acquainted in my career as a biomedical scientist, and which usually can be discussed in plain English.

Let it be clear at once that professional philosophers will have none of me, and *know,* not merely *believe,* that I am truly naive and probably still sophomoric. Yet I've enjoyed my studies, and I believe that I have stumbled onto some ideas, as well as onto some strictly verifiable knowledge of the way in which our brains work, which are generally unknown, or at least ignored, by professional philosophers. These ideas and this knowledge seem so important to me that I want to share it with you, who may read on, or with anyone who may wish to discuss these matters with me. I am from middle class stock: my mother's family having been craftsmen from Solingen, Germany, and my father's folks having been potters from Staffordshire, England. I grew up around Elizabeth, New Jersey, in the conventional school, Episcopal Church, home and yard, typical of the beginning of this century. I was thrilled by Mark Twain's writings, the exploits of Sherlock Holmes, the tales of Rudyard Kipling, and the adventures so well described by Robert Louis Stevenson. This gave me an abiding sense of history and its importance. I also studied chemistry from the Britannica, and was already well enough versed in its details to be able to coach our attractive chemistry teacher, Miss Morris, when I went to Roselle High School. I also acquired an abiding appreciation of music from our friend Thomas Wilson, a considerable authority on Händel and oratorio production.

So I entered the great Princeton class of 1917, and floundered around badly for the first couple of years. The war appalled me. Determining to do my part to make the world safe for democracy, I enlisted in the New Jersey National Guard. Military training was helpful discipline.

At Princeton I was inspired by three great teachers: Edwin Grant Conklin (1863-1952), the distinguished biologist, later my good friend when he was President of the American Association for the Advancement of Science; Norman Kemp Smith (1872-1958), the clear-thinking and clear-speaking Scottish philosopher, and Warner Fite (1867-1955), the thoughtful student of ethical theory. Thus, when I was called into service with the 29th Division to build Camp McClellan, Anniston, Alabama, in March 1917, as top sergeant in a machine gun outfit, these men had already shaped my subsequent intellectual career. But chance ever plays a part in our lives.

The Chemical Warfare Service was being organized, and I

was transferred into it in the spring of 1918. As I learned later, when he was one of my graduate teachers, this was due to Harold Bradley (1878-   ), then Personnel Officer for the Chemical Warfare Service, who noted my biology and chemistry background. He was Professor of Physiological Chemistry at the University of Wisconsin. I was sent there to serve in the medical defense effort against war gases. I studied the blood effects of phosgene, chlorpicrin, mustard gas and Lewisite in morphinized dogs. When the war was ended, my chief, and my revered teacher, Walter Meek (1878-1964), Professor of Physiology, asked me to stay on and run the necessary controls to discover what morphine does. Thus I was launched into a biomedical career.

As an important note, I should add that when Harold Bradley retired, he moved to his boyhood home close to the campus of the University of California at Berkely. Now, in his nineties, he comes over monthly to dinner in San Francisco, with the Chit-Chat club. There I can still enjoy his calm wisdom. He is one of our most influential conservationists.

At the University of Wisconsin I thought first of going into medicine, but, needing money, as I intended to take care of my patient and ever-helpful wife, I decided to get a Ph.D. and enter an academic career of teaching, searching and researching, and rendering what service I could to others. I was ever idealistic, and indeed at one time I had considered becoming a medical missionary.

In addition to Harold Bradley, and Walter Meek, my molding teachers were Arthur Loevenhart (1878-1929), Professor of Pharmacology, Dean Charles Bardeen (1871-1935), Professor of Anatomy, and William Snow Miller (1858-1939), Professor of Histology. I was quite unprepared to discover that none of these fine gentlemen really knew anything about philosophy, although they were training me for the degree of doctor of philosophy. For them, ethics meant merely the Judeo-Christian conventionality; there was merely one logic, a confused jumble of the deductive, inductive and scientific varieties of the various logics, and there was no place at all for the aesthetics.

Yet, there was an opportunity for humanistic endeavor. The austere William Snow Miller had developed a medical history seminar, and I was invited to join. It met monthly in the book-lined library of his home. Each of us in turn was supposed to give a "paper" as an opening for discussion. This stimulated me to undertake a genuine philosophical quest. I was astonished to discover that there was no appreciation among members of the medical profession of the distinction between etiquette and ethics, a potent source of confusion over what is called "medical ethics" among physicians and people generally. So I wrote an essay on "Percival's Medical Ethics" referring to the idealistic effort of Thomas Percival (1740-1804), of Manchester, England. His poorly named "Code" was influential in England and this country for a century. Morris Fishbein, editor of *The Journal of the American Medical Association,* accepted my article and it caught the interest of Harvey Cushing (1869-1939). He invited me to present it at Harvard. This pleased me greatly.

My effort, however, fell flat. When Williams and Wilkins in Baltimore, published my essay in 1927 with a reprinting of Percival's Code, the book was bitterly panned by medical reviewers, chiefly on the basis that since I was not a physician I could not properly appreciate "medical ethics." After several decades this situation changed. I was asked by a potent committee of the American Medical Association, under Doctor Raymond McKeown of Oregon, to advise in regard to a proposal I made, following William Henry Welch (1850-1934), to develop a simple set of guidelines for decent professional deportment.

Thus my interest in ethical theory was aroused. In 1939, when the American Association for the Advancement of Science met at Stanford University, my revered teacher, Edwin Grant Conklin was President. We were now busy developing the Pharmacology Laboratory at the University of California in San Francisco. For our boys' sake, my wife and I got a few acres of redwoods in the Santa Cruz mountains along the San Lorenzo Creek. There on Sunday afternoons we held seminars, after lunch and swimming, under the sheltering

branches of a big red wood circle. We thought to honor
Professor Conklin by asking him to come over.

He did. He came with C. Judson Herrick (1868-1960), the
distinguished neurologist of the University of Chicago, and
Olaf Larsell (1886-1966), the great neuro-anatomist of the
University of Oregon, and previously one of my teachers at
Wisconsin. After an introductory discussion by my colleagues,
Charles Gurchot and Otto Guttentag, contrasting French and
German cultural concepts in the 19th Century, we set ourselves the seminar task of seeing whether or not we could
induce a naturally operating principle among people, which
would have ethical significance. We thought it should be
oriented along Darwinian principles of adaptation as a factor
in survival. The results of our effort were impressive, at least
to me. They are discussed later.

Meanwhile I had accumulated a considerable library of
classic material in philosophy, and I studied it as carefully as I
could. Of course, I missed much. I learned that philosophers
characteristically have trouble trying to communicate in
conventional language.

World War II brought us to Galveston, Texas, to try to
bring the Medical Branch of the University of Texas into some
kind of order and effectiveness for training the health professional personnel so greatly needed. Sporadically I tried to
continue my pharmacological work in developing new drugs,
and to stimulate our students and staff in the history and
philosophy of the health professions.

My publication of an essay called "Ethicogenesis" in the
Scientific Monthly (60:245-253, 1945) brought a sharp critique
from Patrick Romanell, Professor of Philosophy at Wells
College. This resulted in my invitation to him to join our
faculty as Professor of the History and Philosophy of the
Health Professions.

He came and we continued our debate. This culminated in a
small item called "Can We Agree: A Scientist and a Philosopher Argue about Ethics" (Univ. of Texas Press, Austin, 1950,
110-pp.). Later, Patrick Romanell became Benedict Professor
of Philosophy at the University of Texas, El Paso. He is an

authority on Italian and Latin American philosophy. I had aroused his interest in John Locke (1632-1704), whose medical empiricism had, I thought, inspired his philosophical interest. Patrick Romanell is now preparing a definitive discussion on this idea.

My interest continued when we went to the Ohio State University at Columbus in 1955. My effort was now oriented toward theories of ethics in relation to the moral problems now confronting the health professions in abortion, contraception, euthanasia, the right of patients to know the truth, organ transplantation and human experimentation.

When we returned to San Francisco in 1962, I was asked by my friend, Alvin Eurich, then directing the Aspen Center, to participate in one of its general conferences, and in a memorial tribute to Albert Schweitzer (1875-1965). Someone associated with Motorola, Inc., heard me and arranged to have me take part in the vigorous intellectual activities of the delightful Motorola Executive Institute near Tucson, Arizona. There I have been greatly stimulated by the keen staff comprising Doctors William Bakrow, Edgar Cale, and Paul Baker (and "Skip" Berry, the incomparable chef) to organize my ideas substantially as given here. The sessions at the Motorola Executive Institute are really inspiring. Robert Galvin, the President of the Company, has built remarkable morale in his executives by the intellectual program he has so well supported.

These ideas were further explored at a series of discussions arranged by President Walter E. Boek of the National Graduate University at Bethesda, Maryland. In the pleasant informal atmosphere of the Grosvenor Mansion, these sessions were quite provocative.

I am rather naive. I firmly believe, as I said, that individuals getting the academic degree of Doctor of Philosophy, should know something about philosophy. When I was at Princeton, John Grier Hibben (1861-1933), then President, and a well known logician, required all candidates for the Ph.D. degree to attend his weekly lectures on philosophy. Since the lectures were open to anyone who wished to attend, I went to them.

However, I can't say that I remember much about them, except the dullness of syllogistic logic. Yet, Hibben's idea stuck with me.

So, a year or so ago, when I finally thought I had the time, I decided to offer a series of discussions on philosophy to Ph.D. candidates at the University of California in San Francisco. This is primarily a school for the health services and professions, where I had been Professor of Pharmacology from 1928 to 1942. I was also Librarian, and Professor in the History of Medicine. My lectures in the history of the health professions had always been philosophically oriented, and I had discoursed a bit on "medical ethics" and on ethical theories in a more general way.

So, I put up a notice about philosophy talks for Ph.D. candidates, open to anyone. This was very irregular. The course was not approved by any curriculum committee, nor was it catalogued. I told the people who came (some forty, doubling in a while) that they would get no academic credit for attending, but that the effort was honest since I got no money for giving it. It seemed to go well. Maybe it helped by having it at noon and offering cookies and coffee, as bait.

Anyway, it resulted in my being asked to give it for the University Extension. It must have some practical value, for I've been asked to repeat it on many occasions at refresher seminars for busy executives of hard-boiled industrial companies. This book is the result of many such "try-outs."

In a very small way this reminds me of Wittgenstein's slowness to try to get his ideas published. But he was a superbly brilliant logician, and developed a whole new philosophy, somewhat in the mathematical tradition of Spinoza, Leibniz, Newton, Kant and Bertrand Russell. My effort is light years away from Wittgenstein. It is, however, concerned with the practical affairs of living. In this it may reflect a little of Bertrand Russell's desire to share his experience with people, plain, ordinary people, like you and me. Lord Russell's experiences, however, have been fined and refined in the disciplined rigidity of mathematics. Mine are fluid, evolving, and relativistic comments on my experiences with biological concepts. My effort, then, does deal with life - our lives - what are *we* living for?

I've been reading an account of the life and character of that intriguing Austro-English retiring thinker, Ludwig Wittgenstein (1889-1951). This was given me by a young and peppy colleague, Abraham Virdeh, who is interested in the philosophy of the law. My concern with the philosophy of the health professions led me, on one occasion, to try lecturing to law students on medical jurisprudence, so Abe Virdeh and I have had many profitable conversations about philosophy. This resulted in a little essay, "The Strength of Sin Is the Law." (*Lincoln Law Rev.,* 5:5-13, 1969) which Abe published for me.

Perhaps I should study Wittgenstein's reputedly great *Tractatus,* but I cannot get myself to tackle obstruse intellectual treatises. Somehow I want to think about practical affairs of current importance, but in an intellectual manner. I am not an activist. Thus, while I appreciate Wittgenstein's comment that the problem of suicide is the key to all ethical systems, I prefer to contemplate it intellectually rather than consider it actively.

Practical Philosophy: The Ethics, the Logics, and the Esthetics, or our morals, our knowledge and our judgment.

Error of opinion may be tolerated
when reason is left free to combat it.

Thomas Jefferson (1743-1826),
   In Inaugural Address as
   President of USA in 1801

In law one is guilty when one violates the rights of others. In idealistic ethics one is guilty if one merely thinks of doing so.
Immanuel Kant, *Konigsberg Lecture,* 1775

One is moral whose aim or motive may become a universal rule.
R. W. Emerson, *Character,* 1844

To enjoy and give enjoyment, without injury to oneself or to others: this is true morality.
Nicolas Chamfort (1741-1794), in *Maxims,* 1785

Outline of the Discussion

From my personalized account of the origin and development of my ideas about what we are living for, it must be clear that my discussion will not be a conventional one. Indeed, I am quite impatient with "metaphysics." Being a biomedical scientist, I tend to think about specifics.

Thus, in considering the question, *"What Are We Living For?"*, I promptly think of motives, purposes, goals, moods, behavior and interpersonal relations. These I recognize to be matters of psychological and thus of neurophysiological investigation, on which there is much verifiable knowledge.

Hence, my discussion will start with a consideration of the various answers which seem to have been formulated over the long millenia to the basic question of us all, *what are we living for?* The answers are the various ethics. I'll try to review them as briefly as I can (too briefly for philosophical and tiresome analysis, of which I am incapable anyway). This review will be as chronological as I can make it. Here it may be noted that the dictum of Ernest Heinrich Haeckel (1834-1919) seems to apply, namely that the life history of an individual, here a person, recapitulates species evolution, even in ethical theory. This is reminiscent, as suggested by my friend, John Lingenfelder, of that intriguing book, *From Fish to Philosopher* (Harper, New York, 1960) by physiologist, Homer Smith (1895-1958).

All of us at some time ask ourselves, or have to face the asking of ourselves, *what are we living for?* For an individual, this is the basic question, what on earth am I living for? This question has probably been asked by people from the time they began to think. Various answers have been proposed over the millenia of history, and, thanks to the invention of meaningful symbols, whether in ideographs or words, have been recorded. These answers comprise the various ethics, or *moral formulations*.

The basic question of *"what are we living for?"* suggests many related questions, which grow in interest and complexity, as our sophistication increases, either as a species or as an individual.

Some of these related questions are: What guides our conduct?; What are our purposes in living?; What are our goals, in general or in particular?; What governs our behavior?; What motivates us?; What directs our interpersonal relations?; and What determines our moods and behavior? They may all be summarized in asking: What do we want to get out of living, in general, or at any one time in particular.

The various answers, which have been formulated as various theories of ethics, have a long history in the chronology of our species. It is interesting that most of us, consciously or not, repeat in our own individual lives, the recognition of these various ethical theories, as we grow up, as we mature, and as we ruminate on our experiences in living.

Then, whatever may be our goals in general, or at anyone time in particular, we begin to realize by reflection on our experiences, or by "intuition," that we have a better chance of reaching these goals, if we have solid information about them, than if we are naive or ignorant of what factors operate in obtaining them. This raises the problem of the "truth" about ourselves and our environment.

What is actually the "truth" about ourselves and our environment? What is "Truth" in general - or what is "true" in any particular instance? What is the most successful way of getting the "truth" about the necessary basis for obtaining our goals in general, or in particular. What is the "truth" about the value of our goals, or about the means of reaching them? The answers to these questions comprise the various logics, or *methods of reasoning,* which have been formulated over the past centuries. There seem to be relationships here to the various ethics.

Then comes the problem of how most satisfactorily to apply the "truth" about ourselves and our environment to the accomplishment of our purposes, or to reach our goals in general or in particular. How may we most successfully use our knowledge about ourselves and our environment to achieve our desires, or to modify them so that they are attainable? How may we wisely use our understanding of ourselves and our environment to choose goals worthy of being reached, and again for what purposes in general or in particular. The answers, which have been gradually accumulating over the course of our history as a living species, comprise the esthetics, or guides to choices.

These questions involve the problem of judgment. How may we acquire wise judgment? What is wise judgment in general or in particular instances? What is propriety? How do we judge what is fitting or appropriate in our decisions and behavior, and in our moods behind them? What is "taste" and discrimination? The answers seem to continue to involve the esthetics.

What are the arts and the humanities: ends in themselves or means for acquiring judgment? What is the relation of the arts and the humanities to the sciences? Are the arts and the humanities solely vehicles for creativity, or are they useful in understanding propriety and fitness? What is creativity? What is humanism, and may it have value? Again, for what?

While the answers to these questions continue to involve the esthetics, they also seem to be interrelated to the ethics and to the logics. However, the various principles of esthetics do not seem to be as systematically or as successfully formulated as the various theories of ethics or logics. The ethical and logical principles, in being well formulated, seem to have had much more systematic and detailed analysis, critique and characterization than has been the case with theories of esthetics.

The first Hippocratic aphorism of about 430 B. C. remains pertinent: "Art is long, life is short; opportunity is fleeting, experiment is risky, and judgment is difficult."

Consider a couple of illustrations. The general purpose of the health professions is to bring health to sick or injured people, and to keep them healthy. This requires much knowledge of human bodies in sickness and in health, and judgment in applying that knowledge to the accomplishment of those purposes. However, individual sick persons are real tangible

people toward whom physicians must develop firm interpersonal relations in order to achieve the general goal of
getting them well. The individual physician, in each case, must
find out what is the matter with his or her individual patient.
The process of diagnosis requires great skill in judgment and
in reasoning. Then judgment must be made on the probable
outcome of the disease or injury if left untreated. This requires
much knowledge of the natural course of disease or injury,
acquired by experience or study. Always, reasoning by analogy enters into the situation. Then a decision must be made
regarding treatment. From all the plethora of information
available in regard to drugs or surgery, or psychiatry, the
choice must be made of that special particular treatment
appropriate, or fitting, to the particular individual patient in
question.

Here one can readily appreciate the interrelations of attainable goals and purposes with methods of effective reasoning
and with principles of sound judgment. The esthetics comprise the choice of appropriate bits of knowledge, fittingly to
be applied to the accomplishment of whatever purpose one is
considering. The overall purposes, generalized from many
particulars, are the moral choices confronting us, the ethics
from which we may select what path to follow. The information available to us, which to be effective should be verified or
scientific, is the basis for the reasoning we apply to the
situation in order to make effective *the judgment* we use in
applying our *knowledge* to the attainment of our *goals*. Thus,
the ethics, the logics, and the esthetics make an interconnected
triangle of conceptual practicality with which we may satisfyingly cope with ourselves and our environment.

Or consider the building of a bridge, such as the great
Golden Gate Bridge in San Francisco. Here is a clear,
practical problem of great complexity. The purpose is basically utilitarian, which is a well defined ethic. Much verifiable
knowledge is necessary in order that the engineers may
proceed with appropriate plans. Deductive and inductive logic
enter into the planning along with various aspects of the logic
of scientific endeavor, including analogy and statistical analy-

sis. Then extraordinary judgment must be used in applying the verifiable knowledge available to the accomplishment of the purpose. Choices must be made fittingly to apply what knowledge is available to the making of the bridge, from geology to steel technology, from cement and paint techniques to strength of materials, and to environmental steady states. Not only are esthetic considerations involved in this process of planning and construction, but the final result of a useful bridge may be esthetically pleasing. This achievement may then be the source of infinite satisfaction, not merely to the myriad users of the bridge, but especially to its chief designer. It was in fact a supreme joy to Joseph Baermann Strauss (1870-1938), its chief engineer, and the designer of many other great bridges built on the trussion bascule standard.

This is a joy comparable to that which a physician may feel at the successful outcome of restoring a sick person to good health, or that which an artist may feel on the completion of a work of graphic or plastic art, or a musician, or dramatist, or poet, or writer on completing a worthy humanistic endeavor. A mathematician or scientist, whether experimental or descriptive, may get similiar deep satisfaction from the successful solution of a problem or from the discovery of some bit of new verifiable information. This sense of satisfaction, which is strongly conditionable, seems to be what we all seek in living. Further, the drive to obtain it seems to be dependent on primeval built-in mechanisms in our brain stems directed toward self-preservation in regard especially to food-intake, and toward species-preservation with respect to sex activity.

The difficulty with the esthetics is their complexity and the long lack of intellectual organization in their classification, analysis, and discussion. Indeed, esthetically minded people seem to scorn any such approach. Yet, the very matters that seem of paramount importance to our artists and humanists - innovation, invention and creativity - are esthetic derivatives which may profit greatly from intellectual analysis.

My philosophical effort, then, will be concerned with the various ethics, the various logics, and with an attempt at analyzing the various esthetics. Any indication at preference among the various logics, ethics, and esthetics will be the result of my own individual biases, based on my personal conditioning from infancy. This will probably not coincide with the preference of many others. This is to be expected. We do vary enormously among ourselves. As Roger Williams insists, we are each of us unique, not only in genetic constitution but also in conditioning to our varying environments.

Thus it is up to us as individuals, not only to hold a preference for a particular ethic, or logic, or esthetic (to which each of us has been conditioned), but more importantly, to realize that there are actually many ethics, logics, and esthetics, from which to select on different occasions, as our moods shift.

Where then is the consistency? Our desire for consistency (usually expected in others) may simply be a subconscious realization of our own individual inherent and natural inconsistency. Yet even in recognizing our shifting moods and behavior, we can be conscious of some sort of an outside objective standard with which we can measure, at least in part, the significance of what we are thinking and doing. Usually this is the general social mores of our particular group or, more widely, of our tme. Some people, however, try to establish for themselves some sort of an internal subjective standard of behavior. Often this becomes an absolute standard of personal belief and behavior, and may go to various degrees of fanaticism, intolerance, or rigidity. Standards for behavior are practically desirable, but often are difficult to agree upon. In a practical way, our laws comprise such standards. One may say that our laws represent the least common denominator of what we allow ourselves to do without social penalty. Yet some people would have us each set up some inner subjective law which is not to be transgressed without remorse. Consistency can be a very demanding and unpleasant mistress.

The recognition and understanding of the varying and differing ethics, logics and esthetics, may truly be helpful to each of us. This should not be the case merely in knowing ourselves better, but also in an empathetic knowledge of others, as interpreted by conduct and behavior, in addition to discussion with its resulting lip-service. This intellectual appreciation of the various ethics, logics and esthetics may indeed be the key to agapic regard for all people, or any person. Agape of this sort can have very great practical consequences.

So our discussion will begin with a hasty superficial survey of the various ethical foundations, and then go to a rapid review of the various logics, and then to an attempt to analyze esthetic concepts. Before concluding, perhaps we can have a dialogue: readers may insert their opinions and reactions, and look over the discussion as we may try to reach agreement. Here is a worthy ethical objective: to try, as my Wisconsin philosophical friend, Max Otto (1876-1961), would have it, to find what is good and right, not by might, not for its own sake, but by agreement. Toward this end I can be very flexible!

Note: This book deals with the ethics only. Discussions on the logics and esthetics are in preparation. It was felt that a short account of the interrelations of the ethics, logics and esthetics would be appropriate to a consideration of the ethics, since it might help in understanding my opinion as to the place of ethics in a practical philosophical system.

The Ethics

People at their best, like water,
serve as they go along:
like water, they seek their own level, . .
Love kinship with their neighbors, . . .
the right timing of useful deeds.

The Way of Life
Lao-tzu, 7th Cent. B. C.
as translated by Witter Bynner

Morality must justify
itself at the bar of life

Max Otto, in
Science and the Moral Life,
1949

Living things are seekers
and creators, and
striving for goals
is the essence of all life.

Edmund W. Sinnott, in
*Cell and Psyche: The Biology
of Purpose,* 1950.

The Various Ethics, or
Moral Formulations

First, consider the basic questions which at some time or other in our lives, we all face, consciously or subconsciously. Sometimes we may take them seriously, and under adverse conditions, pessimistically. We may go over them in varying detail. Or, when comfortable and content, we may lightly dismiss them and scarcely take heed of them. But, they remain with us; to challenge or to defy us; to tempt our faith, or to reinforce our determination; to annoy us, or to help us to understand ourselves, even at last to defeat us or to aid us to triumph over ourselves.

These basic questions are, to repeat: *What are we living for?* What motivates us? What governs our conduct? What directs our interpersonal relations? What are our purposes in living? What are our goals in living, either in general, or in particular? What guides our thoughts and actions? What shapes our beliefs? What determines our moods and behavior?

The first question is often expressed profanely, with perhaps subconscious realization of the actuality: What in hell am I living for? The last of these questions is a loaded one, and one that only recently are we beginning to understand.

The Concept of the Big Boss

The really basic question, what am I living for, may be answered long before it could be formulated or articulated or even sub- or unconsciously or non-verbally asked. This answer, which we all learn during the first few months of life, is simply to please the Big Boss. Each of us learns this quickly, if we are healthy, on the experience of hope of reward or fear of punishment. Thus it is conditionable from the beginning.

It is during this primary ordering of space and time "out there" as Roland Fischer would have it (*Science,* 174:897-904, Nov. 26, 1971), that an infant structures in its cortex the symbol and signs of the Big Boss as correlated with its chemical development through its mid-brain cell centers concerned with the sensation of hunger and the groping muscle efforts to satisfy that sensation. It is its Mother whom each infant first learns, through the development of hope of reward and fear of punishment in nursing, *is* the Big Boss.

A little later, still as infants, we are likely to learn that one equally to be pleased, in order to receive approval, and to avoid displeasure, is Father. It was not always so. Mothers were the ones who knew that they bore their babies, even though they may not have known which man or what was responsible. Ancient sedentary farming cultures, whether in Egypt, Sumeria, India, China, the mid-East, and in parts of Africa and the Americas, were essentially matriarchal. Only when men learned that they had something to do about where babies come from, did patriarchal cultures develop. The record of the gradual overthrow of the ancient matriarchies by hordes of nomadic horsemen is given in the Greek myths, as indicated so well by Robert Graves (1896-   ), the great English poet. His study of Hebrew myths suggests the extensive editing of the ancient legends which resulted in the Old

Testament as we know it, a rather ambiguous confused mass of patriarchal propaganda.

As children grow older, they learn many other aspects of the Big Boss, the bully of the group, or the teacher in school, or the gang leader. As adolescents they learn who the various Big Bosses are in the Establishment, or in their own rebellious communes. As adults they learn who are the Big Bosses in the community, the State, or the Nation. And always the motivation remains to please the Big Boss in hope of reward or in fear of punishment.

Children also learn to abstract or extrapolate, to the concept of pleasing the Big Boss of everything; that great power in the unknown who can reward or punish in so many unexpected ways. It is significant that the Supreme Big Boss is considered in our culture to be a venerable old male human, and to be addressed as Our Father, or as Allah, the one God. He derives power from the hitherto almost universal belief in an immortality, in which ultimate rewards and punishments are meted out for what socially determined virtues and vices have occurred in living. The basic answer to the basic question of, *"what are we living for?"*, remains to please the Big Boss.

From infancy this matter of living to please the Big Boss is conditionable and transferable for each of us. Social experiences, often shared in common, bring organizational effort directed toward uniform belief and activity, and priesthoods arise, politically and religiously, to enforce such uniformity. The priests become intermediaries between the Big Bosses and their individual constituencies, interpreting what they think will be pleasing to their respective Big Bosses, whether in tribute, in respect, or in obedience.

Various formulations of this Big Boss theory of conduct may be found, mostly legendary from antiquity, and therefore suspect of subsequent editing. Best known in our culture is the Mosaic Code, especially the "Ten Commandments." Already the legal aspects of moral behavior is evident in the implied penalties for disobedience. The Mosaic Code was probably formulated in the 8th Century B. C., when the Pentateuch of the Old Testament of the Jews was edited into its more or less current shape.

A much earlier codification of law governing social behavior was that promulgated by Hammurabi (18th Century B. C.), the 6th of the Amorite 1st dynasty of kings of Babylonia, who set up a remarkably efficient administration. His Code was specific, and operated on the principle of "an eye for an eye." This was the beginning of the legal principle of damage suits. But the Hammurabic Code was entirely secular, while the Mosaic Code claimed divine and supernatural authority, and was clannish in purpose.

It is to be noted that the various chronologically developing theories of ethics tend to overlap, and to show more than vestigial survival. The Big Boss principle governing conduct and behavior remains very much in evidence in racketeering gangs, as the Mafia, and in countries laboring under the weight of dictatorship. It also continues to operate religiously, in Judaism, Christianity, and with Muslims. It is interesting that variations on the theme also continue to show cyclic flowering, as Satanism, witchcraft, and guruism. Some of these, such as witchcraft, have their roots in the ancient matriarchies, as Robert Graves has demonstrated (*The White Goddess,* Faber & Faber, London, 1953, 496 pp.).

Even the patriarchal Big Boss ethos of Christianity had to make concessions to the ancient emotional pull of the matriarchy. The medieval Mary worship was amazingly popular and powerful, in order to please "The Mother of God." It was especially potent in France, as the magnificent Gothic cathedrals to "Our Lady" testify.

It should be clear then that the Big Boss concept has always been a strong motivational force for acceptable social conduct, and even for "righteous" private thoughts of individuals. This basic ethical formulation still operates with us, on the conditionable principle of fear of punishment (the police) or hope of reward (heaven or what happiness is).

The Concept of Responsibility

Some people inevitably mull over intellectual concepts. Often in so doing they become skeptical. They may question the validity of the concept, they may become interested in its origin, or they may be skeptical of its purposes. Thus, it is to be expected that the Big Boss idea as a moral imperative would early be questioned. Our records are not exactly clear, except that secularly, frequent rebellions against the Big Boss of the moment are the stuff of history.

In the religious, and thus in the intellectual, ethical sense, the Big Boss concept was questioned more delicately. It is remarkable that there was temerity enough to bring up the issue of the responsibility of the Big Boss: to mete out punishment or reward justly. It is also remarkable that the concept of justice arose so early.

In our Judaic cultural background, it was the legend of Job which poetically and effectively brought out the idea of the necessity on the part of the Big Boss to be just and responsible, if patriarchically he were to continue to receive respect and obedience. Job's cry that he would continue to trust in "the Lord," even "though he slay me," was a most poignant reminder of the stern and awesome obligation to justify that trust. (Note here the continuing sense of the word "justify"). In the legend, Job's confidence in the justice and responsibility of the Almighty was justified, even after the most terrible of tribulations. Thus the moral of the legend was driven home. Furthermore, the legend indicates that even Almighty Goodness, as God, can be tempted by the spirit of evil, as Satan. But goodness triumphs, both in God and in Job.

What genius was it that in the 4th Century B.C. put the Book of Job together? We have no idea. The character of Job, "a righteous man," was legendary with Noah and Daniel (Ezekiel, 14:14). The concept of responsibility for the justification of trust was already being approached by David, the great leader, who ruled a united Israel for 32 years and died not later than 993 B.C. Often in the Psalms, whether by David or a contemporary, there is allusion to the expectation of responsibility in "The Lord" to justify the trust reposed on him. The two Isaiahs of around 750 B. C. prophesized in the same vein. The Greek myths also began to develop the same theme at about the same time. With the Greeks it was more mundane, and allowed fully for the whims and inconsistencies of people, whether mortal or immortal. Other peoples may have surmised the concept of responsibility, but only vaguely, with little of the majesty or poetry of the *Book of Job.*

The most satisfactory and readily available annotated translation of *Job* is that edited by the Reverend Dr. A. Cohen, dedicated to my friend, Rabbi Henry Cohen (1862-1952), of Galveston, with extensive commentary by Rabbi Dr. Victor E. Reichert (Soncino Press, Hindhead, Surrey, England, 1946, xxx 233 pp.). The *Book of Job* profoundly influenced the mystical visions of William Blake (1757-1827). His *21 Illustrations to the Book of Job,* published in 1826, are his finest artistic work, unequalled in modern religious art for imaginative power.

The ancient problem of the meaning, or meaningless, of life, *"What am I living for?,"* is given a current poetical and dramatic interpretation in *J. B.,* the controversial play of 1957 by our great poet, Archibald MacLeish (1892-   ). In this MacLeish emphasizes a significant moral aspect of the legend of Job. Dramatically portrayed is the transition from a primitive retributive justice, in which distress was considered to be an earned punishment for failing to please the Big Boss, to a more compassionate understanding of misery and hardship. At the close of MacLeish's play, when J. B. is opulent again, but disillusioned, he says to his wife, "what suffers, loves- and love/will live its suffering again." While this is implied in the ancient legend, it is not spelled out.

In developing the concept of the responsibility of God to deal justly, fairly and honestly with people, the commentators on the *Book of Job* seem to have realized the implications of this point of view for their own individual human conduct. This application of the idea of responsible conduct was extended in the Greek myths and in other cultures also to the notion of one's "duty," what one must do to secure reward or to avoid retribution. The idea of duty developed in connection with one's responsibility to one's parents, or to one's children, to one's neighbors, and to one's guests. There was recognition of the obligation of reciprocation in all of this. Loyalty to one's family, to one's group or community, and to one's nation and its ideals and standards, was thus encouraged. The sense of territoriality was an integral part of this development, and gave definite physical meaning to the in-group feeling of loyalty.

Thus from the courageous intellectual feat of skepticism with respect to the consistency or validity of the judgment of whatever Big Boss might be involved, came the developing notions of justifying a trust, responsibility, fairness, justice, loyalty, and even compassion. Significant moral problems relating to beliefs, conduct, and motivation had arisen. Our humanity had grown from infancy into childhood, and, like each of us in a comparable period of individual life, was facing the complexities of adolescence.

The Concept of Sin: the Zoroastrian Dichotomy of Goodness and Evil

The rapidly growing patriarchal ethos was given great and lasting impetus as a result of the remarkably clever influence of the extraordinary Persian sage, Zoroaster or Zarathustra, possibly a chieftain living somewhere between 1,000 and 700 B.C. Already traditional with his people, as indicated by Abbas Aryanpur of Teheran at a recent discussion at the Cosmos Club in Washington, D.C., was deep respect for fire and the sun, and aversion to darkness. This may have reflected the awe felt at the discovery of ways to make and control fire. Zoroaster struggled to establish a solid agricultural state whose laws would encourage stable land use and thrift. He thus repudiated his nomadic background of wandering with flocks. But he kept and expanded his patriarchal behavior which derived from his nomadic ancestry.

This was about the same time that the Jews opted for the culture of flocks of sheep, with all its poetic imagery, against that of farming. This is the point of the story of Cain and Abel: Cain, the "bad guy", was a farmer, who got mad when Abel, the "good guy," allowed his flocks to run over and destroy Cain's crops. So Cain killed Abel, but Abel had the hero's place in the esteem of the sheep-loving Hebrews. It is amazing that now the situation has run full circle. When the modern state of Israel was established in 1948, the first thing the Israelis did was to get rid of all sheep and goats. These had, over the course of centuries, brought the desert, by over-grazing and clogging the springs. Soon the Israelis found the springs opening again, and enough water became available to make Israel lush and green with crops and orchards. At the borders of the country, it looks from the air as if a knife had cut off the green, to let the desert take over. The Israelis offered to help their envious neighbors to get equally green and plentiful crops. But first, the Arabs would have to get rid of their sheep and goats. This they won't do. It's relatively easy to tend flocks as shepherds, but it is hard work to cultivate the land successfully. The Israelis seem to enjoy hard work, and the fruits thereof.

Zoroaster seems to have anticipated the Israelis in trying to persuade his people to cultivate the land carefully. He seems also to have given the ancient mid-east peoples far reaching ideas of "sin" and of "goodness" and "evil." In more simple circumstances, "sin" was considered to be any deviation from the acceptable social norm of conduct for the group. It was to be abhorred by the members of the group, and anyone "guilty" of "sin" would be, and could expect to be, punished in accordance with the severity of the offense. Here was the background for much of law, and for the peculiar psychological conditioning in relation to the feeling and fear of "guilt." This was the common tribal situation all over the earth, reinforced by varying degress of adherence to totem and taboo, as Sigmund Freud (1856-1939) in 1913 so well analyzed.

Zoroaster added the dimension of sex to sin, and thus vastly expanded its significance and importance. This was a forceful facet in the overthrow of the ancient matriarchy by the burgeoning patriarchy. The matriarchy was committed to moon worship, probably because of the correspondence of the 28 day cycle of the phases of the moon with the usual 28 day cycle of menstruation in women. This was no mere coincidence to the ancients.

The matriarchal cultures were fashioned after the example of bees, with the queen as the center of political, material and religious power, ruling through priestesses. Women ran things and men worked under them and pleasured them. Young women were initiated into the mysteries of the matriarchies in special rites which emphasized the inadequacy of an individual and one's salvation in the group. Symbolically it was a second birth, and culminated in ritual drinking of wine laced with the hallucinating mushroom, *Amanita phylloides*. The visions gave a feeling of union with the awesome powers beyond. Such a scene can be noted in the frescoes of one of the rooms in the "House of Mystery" in excavated Pompeii. Such "mysteries" were characteristic of Eleusis and Samathrace in the proto-Greek era.

While the Queen of the clan represented the cyclicly changing moon, she took a consort to represent the sun in its slower cycle of the growing Spring, the blooming Summer, the fruitful Autumn, and the dormant Winter. The lunar cycle was the primitive "year," and there are 13 of these in the annual cycle of the sun. The Queen's consort reigned only for the solar year, and at the end of the 13th month he was killed and his blood used to fertilize the soil. In some groups he was torn to pieces, after being stupefied with wine, by the Maenads, who had excessive strength from wine and the hallucinating mushroom. Probably Theseus was one of the stronger men who resisted this custom, as suggested in Mary Renault's brilliant *"The King Must Die"* (Pantheon, New York, 1958, 330 pp.). This also suggests the reason why he left Ariadne on Naxos.

The matriarchies were gradually overthrown during the second millenium B. C. by nomadic, often fair-haired men from the North, and often on horses (centaurs) or in chariots. These men had few or no women with them. They also seem to have had superior weapons, made of iron, rather than bronze. Over the long centuries of consolidation the patriarchy finally became firmly established; the natural muscular superiority of men putting women to a disadvantage. In many other ways, however, women do seem to be superior to men, as discussed so wittily by my friend, Ashley Montagu, (*The Natural Superiority of Women,* New York).

Then, as the records of these events began to come together in chant and dance, and later in pictographic, syllabic, and alphabetical "writing," editing occurred. This was directed toward justifying the developing patriarchy. Some interesting features resulted. For example, the 5th chapter of Genesis in the Old Testament of the Jews is a clear interpolation. It has little to do with what precedes or follows. It begins, "The book of the generation of the sons of Adam," and goes on to the lengthy "begatting" of a series of men by their preceding men. There is not a woman mentioned. It is, apparently, an editorial effort to indicate the inferiority of women and their non-consequential character. However, the writers forgot themselves: they continued to count lunar cycles, 13 in an annual solar cycle, as years. The result is amusing: Methusaleh was 969 "years" (lunar) at his death, or actually, in solar years, only 74, a reasonable old age for antiquity. Similarly, the Book of Ruth is apparently designed to indicate the proper attitude for women in patriarchal society.

This development of a world-wide patriarchal culture was greatly enhanced by Zoroaster's equation of goodness, doing good, and righteousness, with sunlight, the apotheosis of the sun in a sun-god, and with men. On the other hand, evil, badness, and wrong-doing were equated with darkness, the moon, moon-worship and women. Thus sexual activity, basically associated with women and child bearing, became gradually in itself something evil and bad. Most of the accounts of Zoroaster emphasize the creative opposition of goodness and evil, without realizing the significance of the sexual factor, as in the excellent essay by Karl Friedrich Geldner, the eminent Sanskrit scholar of Marburg (*Encyclopedia Brittanica,* 11th Ed., Cambridge, England, 1911, vol. xxviii, pp. 1039-1043).

Since Zoroaster preceded the time in which the Hexateuch of the Old Testament was edited into approximately its present form, it would seem that his idea of the association of sexual activity and women in the concept of evil and sin influenced the Hebrew myths. While the Garden of Eden as other "paradises," appears to be something derived from the lush visions of those who ritualistically used the hallucinating mushrooms, or *soma,* the myth of Adam and Eve and the forbidden fruit of the tree of knowledge of good and evil seems to have a Zoroastrian background. It is the evilness of Eve, the woman, which brings about the fall of Adam, the man. The myth incorporates the Zoroastrian duality of spiritual forces in that of Goodness (God) in opposition to that of Evil (Satan). This becomes a recurring theme in the Old Testament.

The ancient Chinese emphasizing the origin of life, as they knew it, made the male and female principles, the Yin and the Yang, complementary, rather than oppositional. Thus they symbolized life and its origin in a concavo-convexo line in a circle. The old Egyptians, in symbolizing the same concept in the *crux-ansata,* put the circle for the female uppermost, above the cross for the male. But the Hebrews, probably influenced by Zoroaster, put the male triangle above the female one in the Star of David.

An extreme example of the extent to which masculinity can go in furthering pride, status, honor, triumph and esteem on one hand, or shame, defeat, dishonor, and embarrassment on the other, is given by Clifford Geertz (*Daedalus,* Winter, 1972, *Myth, Symbol and Culture,* pp. 1-35), in his account of "Deep Play: Notes on the Balinese Cockfight." This has significant implications for various games, sports, contests, and gambling with reference to the social control of aggression, hostility and animal fury, by means of "play." These activities are primarily patriarchal, and have been characteristic of all such cultures at all times. Sometimes the stakes in such "play" are high enough to include death to the losers, thus merging "play" with the grim realities of individual combat or warfare. This apparently occurred in the ball games played in the temple-complex ball-courts of Middle America.

The sanctity of the marriage relation grew with social recognition of the necessity of regular and stable provision for the innocent outcome of ordinary sexual activity. Yet it grew under the aegis of male dominance, even to the point of plural wives. It was the culmination of the long and slow process by which men realized that they had as much to do with where babies come from as women, or maybe more. The marriage relation also strengthened the moral force of the sense of responsibility, not only for the welfare of the babies, but also for their place in the tribe.

In spite of the heightened sense of responsibility and of the obligation to justify or fulfill a trust, as reflected in the marriage relationship, the net effect of Zoroaster's genius was to saddle Western humanity with a sexual hangup which we are only now, after three millenia, getting over. According to Zoroaster, the answer to the question of, *"what are we living for?,"* is to do "good," to live a good life, to be righteous, and to avoid doing or countenancing "evil." In this scheme, since "evil" was equated with women and since sexual activity is generally associated with women, any sort of sexual activity is "evil" and is to be avoided. However, compromises of theory with reality are always necessary, so sexual activity for pleasure is "evil," but for procreation is not. This wobbly line has been drawn many times since antiquity, notably by St. Paul, by the 17th Century Puritans, and in Victorian England.

The Tribal Ethic: Promotion of Group Welfare Even At Individual Sacrifice

While familial and clan groups were forming in antiquity, in every part of the world, an important ethical principle was evolving. This, as an answer to the basic question of, *"What are we living for?"*, was simply expressed in the admonition to promote the welfare of the family or group, even at personal individual self-sacrifice. This was a powerful moral force, conducive to family and group survival, and to the material and emotional comfort of their conforming members. It promoted strong in-group loyalties.

It would seem that any action, however vague and non-verbal, with its resultant behavior, which takes into account others beyond oneself, must originate in the family, and specifically in the mother-child relationship. Here starts the Big Boss concept. But it also, reciprocally, involves the ideas of comfort, safety, protectiveness, territoriality, sharing with another, and cooperation. These feelings grow with the physical growth of a child, and in the family milieu they develop into the feeling of belonging to a group. This feeling is enhanced in the changing viscissitudes of the family in adversity, with its individual fear of harm, or in successful achievement, by the family in hunting, shelter, or gathering and sharing food, with its individual feeling of joy in the safety and effectiveness of the family.

In the family milieu, individual children learn quite quickly that they, as individuals, get along more satisfyingly if they cooperate in the family endeavor than if they fail to do so. This socializing force increases within each individual's growth as a member of the family group, and develops into the abiding feeling of family loyalty. In the face of outside threat or

danger to the group or to its territory, this loyalty is enhanced.
By precept and example, each child in a family soon learns
that this family loyalty is rewarding. One learns well before
adolescence that the family as a group, or unit, can get along
better for the benefit of each individual, than if each were to go
her or his way.

These family loyalties move rapidly, by evolutionary extensions to associated families occupying contiguous territories.
The separate families learn in hunting or in defense of home
that co-operation with neighbors is better than competition.
Thus, the clan or tribe develops. The family bonds and
loyalties are extended to the clan. Although we tend to think of
these matters in human terms, many mammals seem to show
similar traits, from whales and dolphins to wolves and
primates.

Some basic biological factors seem to operate in aggrega-
tions of species-related individuals from insects, fish, birds and
amphibia, to mammals with their expanding brains. In spite of
Rudyard Kipling's frank anthropomorphism, what healthy
youngster fails to respond with quickened interest and attention to the tales in the *Jungle Books?* The wolfpack described
therein becomes a working model for a youngster seeking to
know what life is about, and identification with Mowgli
follows almost automatically.

In the milieu of the tribe an adolescent learns quickly that
each member of the group is living for the welfare of the group
as a whole. The adolescents are initiated into the tribe, often
with elaborate ceremony, often sufficiently physical to make a
lasting impression. The rite fully makes it clear that one can
expect nothing but pain until one is accepted into and becomes
part of the social group as a whole. The point is driven home
that each one of the group is expected to do everything
possible for the welfare of the group, even at personal
individual self-sacrifice, if necessary. Every culture has its
legends of its heroes who died defending the territory or lives
of the clan. This extends especially to such dubious groups as
the Mafia or other racketeering groupings. In a real way, this
is the ethic of the "gang."

In a formal intellectual manner, this concept of an individual living for the benefit of the group, was broadly articulated by Plato (427-347 BC) into what has since been known as "social idealism." Sometimes it is referred to as "platonic idealism," but this has varying connotations. Cast in the unusual form of dialogues, the Platonic writings purport to transmit the teachings of Socrates (469-399 BC). But while the embarrassing questioning is legendarily Socratic, the argument in the discourses may be the real Plato. The classical English translation (1891) is by Benjamin Jowett (1817-1893) of Oxford.

In the *Protagoras,* Plato considers self-knowledge and tends to equate knowledge with virtue. But it is in the utopian *Republic* that Plato gives his version of the ideal communistic state, in which not merely individuals as such, but even the families are merged into the social whole, so that children are reared not by their parents, but by the state. The general message is that ideally one is living for the purpose of promoting the welfare of the group to which one belongs, even at extreme personal sacrifice. In much of this Plato appears to be quite dogmatic and moralistic.

So, how about sacrifice? Every USA adolescent knows enough about baseball to understand the theory of the sacrifice hit, which usually advances a runner toward a score, even though the hitter is "out." In this the individual in the team play is expected to sacrifice personal advantage for the success of the team effort. When this is recognized it brings its own glory.

Yet, individual sacrifice for social welfare is a much more serious matter than that involved in play, whether chess or baseball. Historically it often was a matter of individual death, the supreme sacrifice. Religiously it was associated with the common effort to please the unknown powerful Big Boss (or Bosses) "out there." In adversity, whether in warfare, or in plagues or famine, the purpose of the sacrifice was to placate the presumed wrath of the Big Boss. On the other hand, in more regular festivals, its purpose was to try to enlist the power of the Big Boss to give fertility to the lands, to the flocks of domesticated animals, and to members of the tribe. Always, to be effective, the sacrifice must be voluntary, the victim willing. Thus, human sacrifice was ritualized, whether of Iphigenia at Aulus, or of the Mayan virgins, laden with gold and jewels, who leaped into the cenotes of Yucatan, or of the Aztec victims who climbed the steep steps of the temples to have their hearts ripped out.

In the matriarchal Aegean of the "Bronze Age" it seems that the Queen's annual consort, who represented the sun, was sacrificed at the end of the year, in order to fertilize the land and the people. He was either torn to pieces after being made drunk, by the Maenads who were inflamed by wines laced with hallucinating mushrooms, or spread-eagled on an oak tree, emasculated and killed.

Among the ancient Hebrews, a dramatic account is given of the substitution of animal sacrifice for human, when, in the complicated legends about Abraham, he was about to sacrifice his beloved son, Isaac (Genesis 22), and a ram miraculously appeared and was slain instead. The legend indicates how the lad, although curious about it all, offered no resistance. Animal sacrifices to the gods or God now became ritualized. Two interesting consequences developed.

First, while the fat and some parts of the animal were consumed in the flames, some of the meat was ritualistically eaten by the priests, and perhaps by the worshippers, if enough were available. At the slaughter of the victim, some of its blood flowed onto the land to fertilize it, and some was probably drunk by the priests. With the development of totemism, this rite symbolically conferred on its devotees the qualities of the totem animal, eating of which was otherwise taboo. Totemism and taboo were powerful factors in the socialization of individuals in a group, and in their unification.

Secondly, the ritualization of animal sacrifices gave rise to examination of the entrails and carcass of the victim, with the idea of prognostication. If the entrails and carcass were found to be healthy, it was a "good" omen, assuring the pleasure of the gods. But if unhealthy, it was a "bad" omen, foretelling failure, disaster, or sorrow. Among the ancient Babylonians, such divination reached high sophistication, especially in regard to liver, as artifacts testify. Here was the rudimentary origin of an empirical gross pathology. Similarly, in the Aztec ritual, if the heart of the human victim, on being torn from the gashed chest, continued to beat, it was a "good" omen. But if it were quiet it was a "bad" omen, signifiying the displeasure of the gods.

The full significance of individual voluntary self sacrifice for the benefit of all mankind, everywhere on earth, was reached in the development of the dogma of the Christ. According to this, Jesus voluntarily accepted crucifixion as a sacrifice to the Almighty, his and our "Father," for the remission of the "sins" of everyone. By this act, God was supposed to forgive the "sins" of everyone. This remains a central dogma of Christian churches of all varieties, and well illustrates the long social persistence, almost ingrained individually, of the physical significance of personal individual sacrifice for the benefit of the group.

Curiously persistent is another aspect of the ritualized sacrifice, the eating of the sacrifical victim's flesh, and the drinking of its blood. This relates to the rituals of totemism. The rituals involve the incorporation of the qualities or "virtues" of the victim into the bodies and personality of the communicants, and is a prime feature of any sort of human cannibalism. It is amazing in many ways that the ritualistic Eucharist of Christian churches should preserve the essential characteristic of "totem and taboo": the ritualized consumption of that which is otherwise too sacred to be ingested. It is remarkable also that the Roman church has promulgated the dogma that the bread and wine, which Jesus is reputed to have said to eat and drink in his memory, is actually "transubstantiated" at the consecration in the ritual of the Eucharist into the body and blood of the Christ. Sometimes faith can be stretched to its breaking point. Yet, in the "Communion" of Christian ritual, cannibalism is condoned socially, while it is otherwise socially condemned and abhorred.

There is then much to be considered in the moral aspects of social idealism as an ethical theory. Although it developed slowly over a couple of preceding millenia, it was not fully formulated until the genius of Plato could articulate it. Thus, Platonic idealism became the ethical foundation, in its subsequent development, both for Judaism and Christianity. It is thus the basis for the conventional guidelines of "Judeo-Christian Ethic" as followed so widely and often so reflexly today.

Judeo-Christian ethics have a peculiar practical consequence. One of its practical implications is the actual "commune," the group which pools all activities and possessions of the individuals within it, and operates as a social unit, presumably for the benefit of each of the individuals comprising it. When this is extended politically, it is "communism." Amazingly this is anathema to those professing the very Judeo-Christian ethic which inspired it. This difficulty seems to have arisen from the economic consequences and characteristics of communism when applied on a national scale. Judeo-Christian countries are generally committed to some sort of individualistic "capitalism," while the Soviet circuit is committed to some sort of "communism." Actually, the inevitable compromise is evolving, as people understand more fully the various emotional and intellectual conditionings to which they are exposed, or subjected.

Social idealism continues to operate as an evolving ethical principle to which multitudes give service, usually by lip, but surprisingly often by deed. Yet it is usually not realized what its origins were, nor to what its implications and interpretations have gone.

Hedonism: The Principle of Living for as Much Individual Pleasure as Possible

One would expect scepticism to emerge in the development of social idealism, the notion that each of us is living for the purpose of promoting the welfare of the group, even at individual personal sacrifice. Indeed such scepticism did early arise among the Greeks as soon as the impact of social idealism, under Plato, became apparent. The question naturally arose about individual welfare; the dignity of an individual regardless of social grouping, and the happiness of a person without reference to social welfare.

This ethical principle was first formulated by another great Greek teacher, Epicurus (341-270 BC), who established a flourishing school in Athens, where Plato had his "Academy."

Though Epicurus held that personal pleasure is the chief "good," the paramount purpose of individual living, he and his followers led lives of temperance and simplicity. In one of the fragments of his writings, it is said, "When we say that pleasure is the goal of life, we do not mean the pleasure of the debauchee or the sensualist, as some from ignorance or malice represent, but rather freedom of the body from pain and of the soul from anxiety." Materialistically, he held that "when we are, death is not, and when death is, we are not." He influenced Cicero (106-43 BC), Lucretius (99-55 BC), Plutarch (46-120 AD), Pierre Gassendi (1592-1655), and many later English moralists. A current development is given by Robert G. Olson, Professor of Philosophy at Rutgers University, (*The Morality of Self-Interest,* Harcourt Brace, New York, 1965, 182 pp.), although he does not refer to "hedonism."

In seeking freedom from pain, whether physical or mental, and from anguish or anxiety, the hedonistic ethic expresses a longing common to all healthy people. It is interesting that drugs were beginning to be used to reach these goals: wines and beers were known from antiquity to quiet anxiety, and to give some surcease from physical pain. The hallucinating plants, and hemp were used also to quiet anxiety and maybe physical pain. Soon opium, a very satisfactory drug to relieve physical and mental pain, would become widely used. And not only were these drugs used to obtain relief from physical and mental pain, but they were abused, even as now, by some persons to do harm both individually and socially.

Thus there emerged a kind of hedonistic measurement of pleasure and pain, in which the effort was developed of maximizing the former and minimizing the latter, from the position of a given person. This effort became particularly marked much later, in the 18th and 19th centuries, in Great Britain.

For the formulation of social idealism on the one hand, and of hedonism in the other, there was thus a tentative recognition of the clear difference in the organizational level of living material into individuals on the one hand, and social group-ings, or societies on the other. Ancient interest in bees, ants, wasps, and other societies of insects, birds, and mammals increased this awareness. Sacrifical rites, injuries or disease, had forced the dawning consciousness that individuals are composed of still smaller units, the organs and tissues, such as skins, bones, muscles, blood, lungs, hearts, livers, kidneys, stomachs, brains, and so on. This idea of the organization levels of living material, from organs, to individuals, to societies, remained static until the development of the cell theory, by Theodor Schwann (1810-1882).

Considering cells as the basic units of living material, invisible until the technology of microscopy revealed them, Rudolf Virchow (1821-1902) formulated the range of organizational levels from cells to societies. We have extended such levels on the one hand to subcellular units, as membranes, nuclei, mitochondria, microsomes, and so on, and then to molecules, some of which, as the nucleids, comprise viruses and may be crystallized. Here the distinction between living and non-living breaks down, and "death" and "life" are constructs of our experience, as Epicurus implied. And, on the other hand, we have become acutely aware, as a result of the influence of Rachel Carson (1907-1964), that beyond the organizational level of societies, there is the total life of an environment of which humans are merely a part.

In the midst of this range of organizational levels of living material are individuals. In human terms, then, an individual is the prime object of life, and the individual person can (is "free" to) judge how much attention to pay to any other level of organization of living material. An individual person thus becomes the measure of all things, and to that person, pleasure or happiness is the chief "good." This is the hedonistic ethic.

It was generally apparent to sensitive thinkers in antiquity, that there is great variation among individuals and among the organs and tissues of which they are composed, as well as among the social clans into which they were grouped. It is remarkable that it remains quite difficult to extrapolate from what is demonstrable at one level of organization of living material to what may be the case with certainty at another. Thus, it was apparent in antiquity that no matter how much is known of the characteristics of separate individuals, little can be predicted with certainty how they will act as a mob, or any other social unit.

By enhancing the dignity of an individual person, and by

taking a materialistic position, Epicurus sought to diminish fear, especially the fear of death, which he considered to be a major evil; not death itself, but the fear of dying. By emphasizing the desire of each person to achieve as much happiness as possible, he implied the adjustment of people to each other, in order to obtain this individual happiness.

Hedonism, quite like social idealism, remains a powerful ethical force in our various cultures. In general, to live in order to promote the welfare of the group to which one belongs, even at personal individual self-sacrifice, seems to be quite contradictorily opposite to living for the purpose of promoting one's own individual self-interests and happiness, regardless of others. Bluntly, in such extreme terms, social idealism and hedonism are essentially contradictory and opposing ethical theories. Yet, practically, we find adjustments and compromises are essential to getting on with others, and such compromises come, especially as we grow older.

This conflict between the ethical principles of social idealism and of hedonism continues to cause difficulty. As I have repeatedly noted (most recently in *World Medical Journal,* 4: 75-76, 1971), physicians have generally professed a socially idealistic ethic, doing everything possible for sick people, even at personal sacrifice. Leaders of medical organizations stress this with platitudinous regularity, and people assume that this Judeo-Christian ethic is the standard of the profession. But physicians must be able to support themselves and their families in the manner expected of persons in their position. The result is that sometimes physicians develop a displeasing hedonism.

We all like consistency. It is thus painful to discover that "medical ethics" is chiefly a mash of Emily Post guidelines to conduct designed to enhance the dignity, prestige, and position of those physicians within the "Establishment," and to discipline those who transgress the rules. The real moral problems of medical practice, such as abortion, contraception, euthanasia, the right of a patient to know the truth, or to die, and human experimentation, are only recently coming to discussion, thanks to Joseph Fletcher (*Morals and Medicine,* Princeton University Press, 1954, 246 pp).

Social idealism and hedonism are the cultural equivalents in the intellectual life of humanity to what most of us experience, consciously or unconsciously in adolescence. The usual turmoil of adolescence comes from the opposing social and individual "imperatives," whether to opt for living for the benefit of the social group to which one belongs, even at sacrifice of one's own welfare, or even life, or rather to decide, "to hell with all that," and to live for the purpose of getting as much pleasure, and as little pain, as possible.

The Harmony Principle

It is remarkable that an effective compromise between the opposing emotional and conditionable pulls of social idealism and of hedonism should have come so quickly and almost simultaneously in widely separated areas. The compromise, on the basis of living for the purpose of being in harmony with one's self, with one's neighbors and with one's environment was developed at about the same time by Confucius (K'ung Fu-tse, 551-479 BC) in China, by Buddha (568-488 BC) in India, and by Aristotle (384-322 BC) in Greece. It may well have been that Aristotle was influenced both by Confucius and Buddha. The efforts of the two latter suggest that the intellectual drive was recognized in India and China before it was appreciated in Greece. Aristotle, however, gave us the most organized and intellectually developed formulation of the compromise, in his "Nicomachean Ethics."

Characteristic of ancient China was the emergence of a "Way of Life," essentially a compromise between the self-interest of a person and that person's realization of the benefit to be derived from benefitting others. It was a harmony ethic conductive to orderliness and peace. As expressed by the poet-philosopher, Lao Tzu (7th Century BC), in *The Way of Life According to Lao Tzu*, (translated by Witter Bynner, Capricorn Books, New York, 1962, 76 pp):

"People at their best, like water,
Serve as they go along:

Like water they seek their own level,
The Common level of life,
Love living close to the earth,
Living clear down in their hearts,
Love kinship with their neighbors,
   The pick of words that tell the truth,
The even tenor of a well-run state,
The fair profit of able dealing,
The right timing of useful deeds,
And for blocking no one's way,
No one blames them."

Confucius may have derived some of his philosophy from Lao Tzu, and he may have been influential in maintaining a secular character for Taoism. His "Analects" (translated by Arthur Waley, Vintage Books, New York, 1898, 275 pp.) are chiefly maxims and proverbs ascribed to "The Master." There is little recognizable order or sequence among them, but they give the feeling of the wisdom of long experience. As examples, one may quote,

> "The Master said, a wise man (gentleman) takes as much trouble to discover what is Right as lesser men take to discover what will pay." "The Master said, In the presence of a good man, think all the time how you may learn to equal him: in the presence of a bad man, scrutinize yourself within." "The Master said: I have never seen anyone whose desire to build moral power was as strong as sexual desire." "Those upon whom neither love of mastery, resentment nor covetousness have any hold may be called Good."

The Chinese "way" is exemplified in the saying: "When each person in a family is in good order, then the whole family is in good order; when all the families in a community are in good order, then the whole community is in good order; when all the communities in a state are in good order, then the whole state is in good order and when all the states in the world are in good order, then the world is at peace, and there is happiness for everyone." This is the essence of the harmony ethic!

In the 4th Century BC lived another Chinese sage, Mencius. His sayings (D. C. Lau, translator and commentator, *Mencius,* Penguin Books, Baltimore, 1970, 280 pp) are ampli-

fications of those of Confucius, and have greater context. They
were influential in enhancing Confucian morality at a time
when an aggressive legalism threatened. Mencius emphasized
the importance of the "thinking heart," or individual conscience, in moral conduct. It was in the Chow dynasty (1122-
256 BC) that the great Chinese moralists labored. In general
they held to the principle that the best government was the
least: "The more restrictions and prohibitions, the poorer the
people; the more laws and edicts, the more thieves and
bandits." Many of these maxims have the same ring of the
wisdom of experience that we associate with the ancient folk-
proverbs ascribed to Solomon (1015-977 BC?). A brief useful
account of Chinese philosophy has been compiled by Ch'u
Chai and Winberg Chai (Washington Square Press, New
York, 1961, 252 pp).

Gotama, the Buddha or "Enlightened One," taught a three-
fold morality: at its lowest it is selfish, with pain for immoral
living and pleasure as the award of righteous living; then it
rises to a rational basis for goodness in that one person's
goodness raises that of all in the group, and to do evil is to
harm one's fellows, and then the realization that virtue awards
itself. The motives of wrong doing are listed in a practical way
as lust, covetousness, hatred, anger, and fear. One would be
wise to follow the middle way between the extremes of
asceticism and of self-indulgence. This is the Karma, with its
eight-fold way, of understanding; altruism; self-control; correct action and abstaining from killing, stealing, sensuality,
lying, and intoxicating drink or drugs; socially approved
livelihood; effort to prevent evil, remove evil from one's mind,
develop goodness and acquire new goodness; concentration on
goodness ("Yoga"), and self-enlightment.

Unfortunately, much charlatanism has developed in Buddhism, with alleged psychic gifts taught (for fees) by count-
less self-styled Yogis. The specific working of the Buddhistic
morality makes it more of a code of conduct than a broad
ethical principle. Yet its thrust is toward a harmonious
adjustment of one to one's neighbors and surroundings. It is
thus a compromise between a general social idealism and an

individual hedonism. It is well described by Ch. Humphreys (*Buddhism*, Penguin Books, Baltimore, 1951, 256 pp), and in translations by Henry C. Warren (*Buddhism*, Harvard University Press, 1896, 496 pp).

My own opinion is that the "harmony" ethic of Aristotle (384-322 BC) was inspired by reflection on circumstances of his early years. He was born in Stagira in Thrace, where his father, Nicomachus, was an Asklepiad physician to Amynta II, King of Macedon. His father could have been familiar with the Hippocratic writings, roughly contemporaneous with him. The ethical aspects of the Hipprocratic Corpus were likely to have been current in the Greek world for some time. Aristotle himself is reputed to have been taught dissection, and was even accused by Epicurus of practicing medicine. Certainly Aristotle was slanted by his father toward biological interests, as well as court life. Physicians generally are empirically oriented, but, as the Hippocratic writings reveal, were early alert to the deep moral problems confronting them in practice.

At about seventeen, Aristotle came to Athens to study under Plato at the Academy for some twenty years. It is clear that, although loyal, he gradually dissented from the strict social idealism of his master. He may have had discussions with Epicurus. He may have begun to see the possibility of developing a compromise between the Platonic social idealism and the Epicurean hedonism, neither of which had then been so labelled at that time. When Plato died, Aristotle went with friends to Assos, where he admired the efforts of Hermeias, the ruler, to realize the Platonic ideal of the good leader. But Hermias was betrayed to the Persians, who killed him, when he refused to betray his followers. Aristotle wrote a eulogistic poem to Hermeias, in which it was said that Hermeias had demonstrated, as any hero, that goodness in itself is worth dying for. Aristotle married Hermeias' niece, Pythias, who unfortunately died. Later, Aristotle married a woman of his native, now rebuilt, Stagira, by whom he had a son, named Nicomachus, for the Stagirite physician, Aristotle's father.

After living in Mytilone on Lesbos, with his pupil, Theophrastus (372-286 BC), and after tutoring Alexander (356-323

BC), the son of Philip II (382-336 BC), King of Macedon, for seven years, Aristotle returned to Athens. There he established a famed school, the Lyceum, where he taught and wrote voluminously. In the anti-Macedonian feeling in Athens at the death of Alexander the Great, Aristotle retired to Chaleis, where he died the next year. Quite full accounts of Aristotle's life and vast work are to be found in the essays by Thomas Case (*Encycl. Brit.,* 11th Ed., Cambridge, 1911, Vol. 2, pp. 501-522); J. A. K. Thompson (*The Ethics of Aristotle,* Penguin Books, Baltimore, 1955, 320 pp), and J. D. Kaplan, (*The Pocket Aristotle,* Washington Square Press, New York, 1959, 381 pp).

It is usually said that Aristotle's *Nicomachean Ethics* was written to, or for, his son, Nicomachus. It is equally possible that it was written in tribute to his father, Nicomachus, who probably was seen to be struggling with the ever pressing moral problems of medical practice, with its close contact with the lives and deaths of patients and their families and friends. Aristotle was clearly a sensitive intellectual and his careful analysis of moral problems indicates his full familiarity with them in a practical as well as theoretical manner. His *Nichomachean Ethics* may embody many of the moral ideas of his father, Nicomachus, the court physician in Macedon, as resulting from the experiences of his medical practice, in which moral judgments are continually made. The psychological aspects of it all indicate the keen observational powers likely to be found in a successful physician. Perhaps the title, *Nichomachean Ethics,* means that the treatise represents the moral principles of Nichomachus, the physician, as recalled and reflected upon by his son, Aristotle, the philosopher.

It seems that the *Nicomachean Ethics* is an elaboration and development of two earlier ethical outlines by Aristotle, *Eudemian Ethics* and *Magna Moralia*. These latter may have been student notes. The *Nicomachean Ethics* is a full treatise, but not complete in itself, as it goes into *The Politics*. It is arranged in two parts. The first deals with goals, purposes, and ends, and starts out by stating that "the good" is that at which conduct aims, and that ethics is a branch of politics. The second considers virtue, and one's disposition to act "rightly."

The third treats of responsibility and the fourth of liberality. In the fifth, "justice" is viewed as a compromise, a mean between extremes, and in the sixth is expressed the principle of "nothing to excess" and "moderation in all things," a reflection perhaps on the Greek tendency to go to excesses. The seventh deals with inconvenience. The eighth discusses "philia," not merely agapic friendship, but also the family sense of love, and sensual or sexual love. In the ninth is a consideration of service, its valuation and its repayment. Here the reference remains friendship, goodwill, and "homonia" or unanimity and concord.

It may be here, in the problem of repayment of service that Aristotle was thinking of his father, Nicomachus the physician. The matter of physicians' fees has always been a sticky one. Aristotle quotes one of the rules of Hesiod, the 8th Century BC Greek poet.

> "Even with a friend let his reward be fixed beforehand, and thereafter paid in full."

The tenth part takes up the difference between pleasure (of the senses) and happiness (of the intellect), and concludes that the highest happiness is in gentlemanliness, combining virtues and goodness to honor, in the speculative life of intellect. It also includes the practical life of combining prudence (for oneself) with virtue (regard for others) which requires habituation, which in turn requires law, which requires the art of legislation, which requires an understanding of politics. Thus Aristotle's Nicomachean ethics goes into politics, and its thrust is like that of Confucius and the Buddha, toward a life of harmony with oneself and one's surroundings. In reference to the ontogeny-phylogeny relation, the harmony ethic is a reflection of late adolescence, when the rival pressures of winning praise for doing for others and of doing for oneself are harmonized in a realization of the necessity of each, if one is to obtain long-range happiness.

One important aspect of ancient ethical formulation was the inauguration and growth of specific moral guidelines for physicians and pharmacists. Such ethical codes as arose for the guidance of early Chinese and Hindu physicians were directed

more toward enhancing the dignity and status of the prac-
titioners than dealing with basic moral conduct. Thus, they
stipulated much on personal cleanliness, neatness of apparel,
gravity of deportment, and prudence in language. This was
clearly designed to give a favorable image to a physician.
Among the later Muslims this same sort of advice was given to
pharmacists.

Genuine moral standards for those caring for the sick were
first promulgated by the Hippocratic physicians at Cos in the
5th Century B.C. They formed a tight society, the Aesklepiads, taking the position that they were sons of Aesklepios,
the revered god of healing, mythologically the son of Apollo,
the sun-god, whose shafts could both hurt and heal. The
Aesklepiads must have had an initiation ceremony, during
which the neophytes took an oath binding them to the moral
standards of the group. This has survived as the Hippocratic
Oath, still taken, in modified form, by graduates from most
medical schools in the world.

This oath is relatively simple and direct, and it certainly has
been, for centuries, a potent force for righteousness among the
health professions. It stipulates that the initiates will respect
and honor their teachers, and that they will be responsible for
their students; that they will use their ability to help the sick,
and that they will abstain from harming anyone; will not give a
lethal dose of a drug to anyone, nor make such a suggestion;
will not give a woman "means to procure an abortion"; will be
chaste and devout in their lives and practice; will never intend
to do harm or to cause injury; will not abuse their position to
indulge in sexual contacts "with the bodies of women or of
men, whether they be freemen or slaves," and that they will
tell no one what they see or hear, professionally or privately,
that should not be divulged.

Here was a clear statement of the responsibilities of
physicians toward their patients, and was in general accord
with an altruistic ethic and with social welfare. It seems to
have assumed willingness on the part of physicians to forego
personal pleasure in order to do everything possible for the
welfare of their patients. The Hippocratic Oath was Christian-

ized by the Church without altering its major tenets. There was added, however, a rather silly phrase about not operating, "not even for the stone." This reflected the Church's attitude that its clerics, the only ones with learning enough to be physicians, should not operate or shed blood. Thus was surgery divorced from medicine, to the long disadvantage of both.

The relatively high ethical standards of the Hippocratic physicians were favorably commented upon by the Romans and later by the Muslims. Actually they had been extended by the Hippocratic writers to include such short treatises as *Law*, *Decorum* and *Precepts*. These added the admonitions to call a consultant if in doubt and to be reasonable in fees. The Hippocratic ethical position has been well discussed by W. H. S. Jones in *The Doctor's Oath* (Cambridge, 1924, 96 pp.)

Martin Levey has carefully considered the medical ethics of medieval Islam (*Trans. Amer. Philosoph. Soc.,* n.5, 57:pt. 3, 100 pp., 1967). Writing especially of the 9th Century al-Ruhawe, Levey indicates how the Muslims were concerned about the interpersonal relations of nurses, physicians, pharmacists, and physicians. From the great Roman physician, Galen (130-201 AD), who wrote a treatise on *The Passions of the Soul,* al-Ruhawe took the tenets of the Aristotelean moderation and temperance, and the control of passions or emotions by training. It seems that al-Ruhawe's ethical admonitions for physicians were part of the general moral position of the Islamic culture.

There were many later developments in "medical ethics" not the least of which was the Emily Post set of rules of etiquette for physicians, surgeons, and pharmacists, unfortunately called a "Code of Ethics," by its gentlemanly 18th Century English compiler, Thomas Percival (1740-1804). This led to much confusion between mere etiquette on the one hand and problems of real ethical theory and judgment on the other. This confusion continues. I have perhaps written too much about it, and thus with little avail. (*Percival's Medical Ethics,* Williams & Wilkins, Baltimore, 1927, 302 pp.); *Journ. Amer.*

Med. Asso., 208:842-847, May 5, 1969; *Ann. N. Y. Acad. Sci.,* 169: 388-396, 1970, and *World Med. Journ.* 4: 75-76, 1971).

In concluding this discussion of the "harmony ethic" of the ancient Chinese, of the Buddha, and of Aristotle, it may be said that it continues to be very influential in compromising the pull of social organization toward acting for social welfare with the drive of each individual toward personal pleasure. The "harmony ethic" seems to be the ideal toward which democratic governments strive. It is an ethic conducive toward cooperation rather than competition among governments as well as among individual people. It is an ethic of peace.

The Ethic of Stoicism

When Athens and the Greek world succumbed to the power and efficiency of Rome, the relatively diverse moral guidelines, which had been debated, were supplanted by a practical ethic of facing reality with fortitude. This began with Zeno of Citium (342-270 BC), from Cyprus. He and his followers discoursed on the Stoa, the frescoed porch on the north side of the market place of Athens, and hence were called "Stoics." These hard-headed thinkers came from all over the mid-east, and their thoughts expressed east-west interactions following the conquests of Alexander the Great. Their contributions are well analyzed by Robert D. Hicks (*Encycl. Brit.,* 11th Edition, Cambridge, 1911, vol. XXV pp. 942-951).

Influenced in part by the harmony ethic of Aristotle, they tended to emphasize the dignity of individuals against the potential injustice and inequities of society. Stoicism reached its high point in Rome, "where the grave earnestness of the national character could appreciate its doctrines." It formed the creed of some of the best of Roman thinkers, such as Lucius Seneca (the younger, 5 BC - 60 AD), Epictetus (50? - 3 AD) and Marcus Aurelius Antoninus (121-180).

Beginning as a cynic, Zeno was a frank materialist, opposing Platonic idealism, and while individualistic, he seems to have doubted personal pleasure as the goal of living. He thus was following Aristotle in seeking a middle way between the push of social welfare and the pull of individual hedonism. His successor, Cleanthes (300-220 BC), noted tension in all things and activities, which in a Heraclitean echo, gives flux and variety to everything. In a Zoroastrian echo, he taught that all vitality and force on earth comes from the sun. His Hymn to Zeus is a noble expression of awe in the face of the power and mystery of the universe about us. His follower, Chrysippus (280-207 BC), well summed up the ethical position of the Stoics.

According to the Stoics, goodness lies in understanding "nature," one's own and the environment about one. Evil remains the result of ignorance. A wise man will live in conformity with nature, and have self-control whether in success or in misfortune or pain. While errors often may corrupt nature, the wise person will understand such errors, and live above them, or suffer them with equanimity. The Stoics denied pleasure as the main goal of human activity, and insisted that virtue is its own reward, and its own good. Pleasure is merely the accompaniment of virtuous activity. They tried to formulate a way of consistency in one's activities.

In Rome, stoicism was put into actual practice as a standard of behavior. Seneca of Cordoba in Spain emphasized the dignity and worth of each individual, with the sense of internal freedom that comes from self-examination. He urged calm resignation to fate, and justified suicide. This was his own fate. Robin Campell has translated and edited selections from Seneca's 124 letters to Lucilius, the first real "essays" (*Seneca: Letters from a Stoic,* Penguin Books, Baltimore, 1969, 254 pp., with admirable notes). Epictetus, originally a slave, left no writings, but a pupil, Arrian, collected his sayings in a book entitled *Enchiridion.* His teachings centered around forbearance and understanding of oneself and others, and he advocated cheerfulness in accepting the inevitable. His was a teaching of live and let live, to bear and forbear. He had a practical turn of mind, perhaps related to his experience as a slave.

Here it should be realized that in Graeco-Roman times a slave was considered to be a human being, worthy to be treated as such, and if worthy enough, to work out or be granted freedom. This is in marked contrast to the Anglo-Saxon concept in which slaves were considered to be mere chattels, no more worthy of consideration than special beasts of burden. This distinction complicated the slavery situation in the USA, and was responsible for much of the difficulty over it.

The well-known writings of Marcus Aurelius, the Roman Emperor of the 2nd Century of our era, seem to represent a transition from a stoical ethic of self-assurance and individual pride to an almost Christian ethic of humility. This may reflect the change from the serene peace of the Roman empire to the time when increasingly plagues, famines, and border invasions threatened everyone's security. There was a strong religious motivation in Marcus toward self-mastery and responsibility in what he considered to be his duty on behalf of the people of his Empire. This all opened a way for the growing success of Christianity. Indeed, Maxwell Staniforth, in his introduction to his translation of the *Meditations of Marcus Aurelius* (Penguin Books, Baltimore, 1964, 188 pp.), says that Stoicism is a very root of Christianity. So, its maxims and precepts were absorbed into a great and lasting complex, religiously oriented.

The Ethic of Compassionate Understanding
Jesus and Hillel

Any rationally satisfying discussion of the tremendous impact on ethics of Jesus must take into account both the historical Jesus and the legendary Christ. This is a matter beyond the interests either of current "Jesus-freaks" or commercially slick entrepreneurs who thrive on the vulgar garish spectacle of "Jesus Christ, Superstar." The historical Jesus seems to have been an Essene, a member of an ascetic sect. He seems to have absorbed the teachings of the sect, as well as those of Hillel, the Babylonian (60 BC - 10 AD), one of the greatest teachers of Jewish law. Hillel, when about 40, came to Palestine and became head of the Sanhedrin, the ruling high priests of Israel. Jesus may well have become imbued with a Messianic urge, reflecting the intense desire of the Jews to be free from bondage to Rome. The historical Jesus may indeed have made enough trouble for the authorities to be condemned to crucifixion. And indeed he may even have been taken from the cross while yet alive, to be returned to his Essene sanctuary. Writings about the historical Jesus include that of Albert Schweitzer, *The Quest of the Historical Jesus* (Macmillan, New York); George Moore's novel, *The Brook Kerith* (Macmillan, London, 1916), and that amazing novel, *King Jesus* (Universal, New York, 1956, 383 pp.) by Robert Graves.

Graves takes the position that Jesus, born of Antipater, son of Herod, and Mary, was legitimately King of the Jews by two lines of descent. Antipater and Mary were secretly married. Herod killed Antipater, and Mary already with child by Antipater was espoused to Joseph. Graves spoils his tale in part by a peculiar lapse: he has Mary writing to Antipater in a code used by many more recent adolescents, the use of chapters and verses of books of the Bible from which the message is deduced. The difficulty is that the numbering of chapters and verses in the Bible was first done in our 16th Century by Robert Estienne (1503-1559) to aid readers in ready biblical reference. Graves pictures Jesus as a determined woman-hater, who thought at first that he might restore the Jewish kingdom, but who belatedly realized it could not be of this world. Graves' historical commentary on his novel, while suggesting profound scholarly erudition, is more confusing than helpful.

The legendary Christ has well edited documentation, not only in the canonical books of the New Testament, but also in a great amount of apocryphal writing. None of this is strictly contemperaneous with Jesus, but began a generation or so after his death, when the anticipation of his return to rule his kingdom had worn off. The legends then began to be edited to conform to the idea of a kingdom of goodness and peace, not of this world, but of the spirit. There is evidence of much dissension among the early Christians, as Oscar Cullman has shown (*San Francisco Chronicle,* March 18, 1969). The legendary Christ is superbly and succinctly pictured in the "Creeds," those statements of belief professed proudly by the growing numbers of Christians.

The creeds seem to have originated in the polemical debating in Alexandria between the Christians and the Hellenistic philosophers known as the Neo-platonists. The Christians were at an intellectual disadvantage in claiming one God only but then claiming that He has a divine Son. The rationalists seem to have been routed by the invention of a deliberate mystery, the Trinity, Father, Son, and Holy Ghost, as something to be taken on faith, regardless of reason. The Christian leader in this development was Athanasius (296-373), but he was opposed by Arius (260-336) who denied the dogma of the Trinity, and asserted that Jesus was a man and no more divine than other people. This difference of opinion made trouble all over the growing Christian world. Flavius Valerius Constantinus (274-337) had become Roman Emperor, and having been converted to Christianity, gave civil rights and tolerance to Christians in the edict of Milan in 313.

But dissensions in the growing church caused Constantine to call the great Council of Nicea in 325 so that the bishops might decide once and for all what a Christian was to believe. The Council was a stormy one. Troops were brought to keep order. Word for word the great Nicene Creed was hammered out. The Trinitarians won. The Unitarian doctrine of Arius became heresy, and gradually the Arians moved eastward. By the 6th Century they seem to have been well established at Ghandiza-pur in Persia, with a flourishing intellectual effort based on the Greek classics which they brought with them. One of their groups, the Nestorians, even taught as far eastward as China. In the 7th Century came the poetical Mohammed (570-632) who fired his followers with his simple faith in one God, making the Moslem state and church one from the time of the Hegira in 622. Thus, the basic doctrinal and political clash between Christianity and the Moslem world began in the dispute at the Council of Nicea between the Trinitarians under Athanasius, and the Unitarians under Arius.

Athanasius seems to have developed a relatively straightforward statement of belief for his Christian followers in a creed embodying the doctrine of the Trinity, the Virgin birth of the Christ, and the resurrection of the body. Speaking of Jesus, the "Apostle's" or Athanasian creed says, in the standard *Book of Common Prayer,* (Oxford University Press, New York, 1938, p. 15), "Conceived by the Holy Ghost, Born of the Virgin Mary; Suffered under Pontius Pilate, was crucified, dead and buried; He descended into Hell; The third day he rose again from the dead." But the Nicene Creed (Ibid. p. 16) speaking of Jesus, says, "was made man; and was crucified also for us under Pontius Pilate; He suffered and was buried; and the third day He rose again according to the Scriptures." It is rather astonishing that the carefully wrought Nicene Creed makes no mention of Jesus dying.

I have called this discrepancy to the attention of many prelates, getting polite smiles in return. When I described this difference recently at a session at the great Catholic University in Washington, D. C., a pert and pleasant nun said, "OK, we changed that." She thereupon showed the recently Church approved Mass in which the Nicene Creed now includes the word "died," as in the Apostle's Creed. Here is a remarkable example of current editing of material to fit a purpose.

We have no extant copies of the document originally wrought at Nicea. But the legendary Christ had been established, and the legend became dogma, later to be embellished and adapted to changing times and popular needs, as in the case of Mary worship, of the adoration of and reliance on saints, and even of acknowledgement of the power of evil personified in Satan. Thus developed the Christian pantheon, while the Moslem faith remained monotheistic.

Whether we consider the historical Jesus or the legendary Christ, the moral impact is much the same, although in the latter case it is reinforced by religious conviction. In general, in association with what we have of Hillel, an Essene leader, the ethical thrust of Jesus was righteousness by precept and example, even extending to righteous indignation, as in clearing the Temple of money lenders. It was an ethic of living for the purpose of benefiting others, and in doing so with compassionate understanding. This implied understanding of oneself and one's motives, as well as understanding and compassion for others. The Judeo-Christian ethic was thus an extension of Plato's ideas and of social idealism to include the emotional force of compassion, of empathy, of sympathy, and of pity.

A tendency of the Judeo-Christian-Muslim ethic was toward asceticism, toward individual self-control, manifested in restrictions on personal indulgence or pleasure. There was thus emphasis on the evil character of gaming, alcoholic beverages, and licentiousness of any sort. This was an effective reaction against the frequent excesses of the Romans. There was increasing regard for the welfare of the poor, the oppressed and the unfortunate. At first there was little condemnation of sexual pleasure, as long as the rights of the innocent consequences were respected. Adultery was frowned upon. The Muslims permitted a circumscribed polygamy as long as all of one's wives were cared for. In general, the Judeo-Christian-Muslim ethic was strongly patriarchal, and a Zoroastrian mist of evil still hung around women.

The Ethic of Sex-Oriented "Sin"
St. Paul

For the Christians, Saul of Tarsus (1st Century A. D.) inaugurated the concept of the inherent sinfulness of sexual activity. An epileptic, who in a characteristic epileptic aura saw "the light," Saul became an almost fanatic Christian, taking the name of Paul, and preaching and developing the legendary Christ. He was a vigorous organizer and travelled around the mid-east, founding churches, and writing to the various Christian groups to expound the "gospel" as he saw it. Some of his famed epistles antedate the accepted Gospels.

He had a pronounced patriarchal disdain for women and

seemed to be "hung up" on the idea that sexual activity is the acme of "sin." The only justification for sex was said to be procreation, although according to him, sex acts are "impure." His ethic was a genuine "puritan" ethic. He gave it a powerful religious slant, and had much to do with developing the "divine authority" of the scriptures as supernaturally inspired. Certainly Paul was inspired. He wrote brilliantly, with sharp metaphor, and clear simile. He probably dictated, often so rapidly that his scribe could not catch up with him. Thus, in the famed 15th Chapter of II Corinthians, where Paul was inspirationally teaching the glories of faith, hope and "charity," there occurs a remarkable definition: "The strength of sin is the law." As I showed (*Lincoln Law Review,* 5:5-13, 1969) this makes no sense. What probably was said was "The strength of sin is what makes the law necessary," but his scribe did not get it all down.

Paul faced many tribulations and much dissension. Yet his teachings prevailed, and the Christian Churches started under him to promote the legendary Christ in the manner later established in the Nicene creed. With state support of Christianity, the ancient pagan glories of the Graeco-Roman world faded. This was especially marked in the sudden collapse of the worship of Asklepios or Aesculapius (of the Romans). There were elaborate precints and temples in his honor, as the great healer, the popular savior of the sick. Some 80 were scattered about the Hellenic world, with exceptionally fine Asklepia, as they were called, at Epidaurus, Pergamon, Athens, Delphia, Cos and Ephesus. These were usually located near a healing spring, and the grounds included the temple, places for the temple-sleep, baths, gymnasia, libraries, race courses, and superb hillside amphitheaters. These were all part of the therapeutic ritual. It was in these theaters that the great tragedies of Aschylus (525-456 BC), Sophocles (496-405 BC) and Euripides (484-406 BC) were performed along with the bawdy comedies of Aristophanes (448-388 BC). All of these inspired strong moral feelings encouraging fortitude, righteousness, loyalty, forebearance, gratitude and piety. They are still produced with telling effect, and even in the millenia old amphitheater with its marvelous acoustics, at Epidaurus.

Strangely, not a vestige remains of the Asklepia, except the hillside theaters. This is peculiar, since many of the temples of the various communities still stand. The Asklepion at the side of the Acropolis in Athens is gone, but the temples on the hilltop still stand, in spite of earthquake and gunpowder. It seems that the Asklepia were deliberately razed, apparently by the Christians of the 4th Century AD, who could not tolerate a rival savior to Christ the Savior. Since snakes were the symbols of Asklepios, this may explain part of the fulminations in the Book of Revelation against "that great snake," the Antichrist that must be destroyed. The efforts of Julian the Apostate (331-363) were of no avail, and the legendary Christ triumphed completely. Dimitri Merezhkovski (1865-1941) has given a vivid impression of the time in his brilliant novel on Julian, *The Death of the Gods* (Modern Library, New York, 1929, 473 pp., translated by B. J. Guerney).

Having established the legendary Christ, Paul and his followers laid the foundation for the huge and magnificent writings in justification of Christianity and its rigorous ethic. In considering Socrates (Plato), Buddha, Confucius and Jesus, Karl Jaspers (Harcourt, Brace, New York, 1962, 104 pp.) comments that in common they had originality and a life at their own risk, and that they became models for humanity, realizing the human situation and showing ways to meet it. In reality, however, none of us can really follow them. Paul showed a moral path to possible inner individual peace, but it was at the expense of the historical Jesus, and based on blind faith in the legendary Christ.

The Ethic of Authoritarian Rule
The Monastic Ethic: Obedience

The decay and dissolution of the Roman Empire left Europe in chaos. Pestilence, filth and squalor was the common lot, along with famine and violence. The Muslims swept over Asia Minor, North Africa, and into Spain, supporting a rich, luxurious, splendid and well-organized culture. In Europe only monasteries and convents afforded refuge and shelter from the surrounding misery. In them rose a well-organized system based on disciplined adherence to practical rules for orderly conduct and communal benefit. When Charlemagne (742-814) brought some general order from the chaotic conditions prevailing, the disciplined rule of the monasteries was extended to fortified walled towns for group safety and the feudal culture arose.

As Oxonian Henry Hubert Williams put it (*Encycl. Brit.,* 11th Ed., Cambridge, 1911, Vol. IX, pp. 808-845), the distinctive features of medieval Christian ethics were obedience, unworldliness, benevolence, purity, and humility. A specially codified morality made obedience to authority mandatory under threat of punishment. Specific rules of conduct as in the monasteries, inculcated the feeling of guilt, if broken, and this could be relieved by confession, repentance and penance. The threat of excommunication, expulsion from the security and comfort of the in-group, would become a major factor in enforcing obedience, and in maintaining unity of faith. Codified ethics could, and did, degenerate into a set of guidelines for conduct and behavior acceptable to the group, often with etiquette supplanting ethic.

The European medieval communities fostered a Christian ethic stoical in its professed scorn for wealth, luxury, fame, power or possessions. Yet this ethic promoted a practical benevolence, exalting agapic love as the greatest virtue. Among the troubadours of southern France this exaltation of agapic love could take a carnal twist, bringing trouble. The prevailing authority called for an inner purity, especially in sexual affairs, advocating chastity, the sanctity of marriage, and sexual union for procreation only, never for pleasure. However, there seems to have been plenty of thumbnosing at the pompousness of the guardians of the Establishment. But humility was fostered, and too often was worn as a cloak, thus generating a conscious hypocrisy. True humility was realized to result from detailed and merciless self-examination. This was the worthy moral ideal. Often it came in the recognition of the futility of an early life of "wild oats" with excesses of self-indulgence, as in the case of Francis of Assisi (1181-1226).

The Medieval Christian ethic was given much of its position by the influence of Ambrose of Milan (340-397). His fairness in the Arian disputes brought him the bishopric of Milan. Giving all to the poor, he won wide respect, especially for his severity against wickedness, even in high places. He refused entrance to his church to the Emperor Theodosius (346-395), a relatively enlightened Trinitarian, because of the massacre of rebellious Thessalonians, excommunicated him, and restored him to grace only after severe penance. The long struggle between the Church and Emperor had begun, and as long as the Emperor still believed, especially in an afterlife, the Church prevailed. Ambrose inaugurated the characteristic rituals and chants of the Church, thus providing a most effective way of teaching its dogmas.

Augustine, Bishop of Hippo in his native Numidia (353-430), was a favored pupil of Ambrose, and was a reformed rake, as his *Confessions* (397) indicate. This was the first autobiography, and was brilliantly introspective and psychologically subtle. His *City of God* (413) remains a justification of the Christian Church as a new order or way of life, built on the remains of the Roman Empire. Augustine recognized his many mistakes, and in 428 issued his *Retractationes*. His main ethical thrust was reliance on God, the supreme ideal of goodness, and on agapic love, with "sin" conquered by faith. He prevailed against the "Donatists" who claimed independence from the Church, and he defended the orthodox unity and authority of the Church. Although having once embraced the "Manicheans," who revived the Zoroastrian doctrine of the dualism of evil and good, Augustine put them down by arguing that the omnipotence and goodness of God makes the existence of a spirit of evil impossible. The third century revival of the Zorastrian dualism of the joint powers of good and evil, in the Christianized version of Mani, the martyrized Persian sage, finds a curious echo currently. In a perceptive essay, *"On Dualistic Thinking: From Mani to the New Left"* (University, #44, Spring, 1970), Walter Kaufman of Princeton says, "It is time to move beyond black and white and to start thinking in color." His point is that our New Left, like the Old

Right of the Nazis or Birchers, sees everything in terms of black and white, whereas in reality most everything is some shade of gray.

Against the "Pelagians" who believed that people could find "heaven" by moral effort, Augustine emphasized "original sin" in the nature of people, and the arbitrariness of grace, merited by none, but granted or withheld by God. In his essay, *"Of True Religion,"* (trans. J. H. Burleigh, Regency Co., cago, 1959, 107 pp.) is his dictum, *Credo, ut intelligam,* "I believe, in order that I may understand."

Yet Ambrose and Augustine did much to codify the Christian principles. There soon was current the notion of the four "cardinal virtues": Christian Wisdom, of faith in God; Christian Fortitude; Christian Temperance and Humility, and Christian Justice with all sharing in a community of benefits. These were balanced by various sins, the venial ones of which could be forgiven by prayer, alms giving and fasting, and the "seven deadly sins" of Pride, Avarice, Arrogant Anger, Gluttony, Sexuality, Envy and Indifference, which required evidence of repentance by severe penance. These were expressions of the monastic moral experience. Murder, theft, assault and rape were dealt with summarily.

An important ethical aspect of the rising Christianity was its anti-intellectualism. It was eagerly embraced by the common people who could no longer keep up with the intellectual discussions on philosophical problems, or with the dawning scientific reasoning of such as Aristotle, Aristarchus (about 264 BC), Archimedes (287-212 BC), Hippocrates (460-377 BC), Hipparchus (about 125 BC), Euclid (about 300 BC), Eratosthenes (276-194 BC), and Galen (130-201 AD). Alexandria was the center for the new scientific effort in mathematics and astronomy, as well as for human anatomy and physiology. It also was the center for violent religious disputes. The Christians being generally anti-intellectual, were against the new knowledge in mathematics and astronomy. The feeling ran particularly high against Hypatia (d.415), not only because she was a brilliant mathematician, and Aristotelean, but also because she was a beautiful woman, and thus intrinsically evil to them. She was hacked to pieces by a Christian mob excited by the fulminations of a Christian demagogue against heathen practices. No significantly helpful formulated ethical principle emerged from the intellectual turmoil except perhaps the asceticism of Plotinus (205-270). There were, instead, quite unpleasant examples of the emotional excesses of irrationality.

The transition from the classical Greco-Roman ethical positions to the unity of medieval European morality was marked especially by the poet-philosopher Boethius (480-524). Although enjoying for long the favors of the Ostrogothic Emperor, Theodoric (455-526), Boethius incurred enmity by his strictures against the Arians, and was imprisoned and beaten to death in Pavia. While in prison he wrote his *Consolation of Philosophy* (translated and introduced by V. E. Watts, Penguin Books, Baltimore, 1969, 188 pp.), a remarkable dialogue, with poetical interludes, with an attractive imaginary woman representing and called "Philosophy."

Morally, Boethius indicated that the supreme good is general happiness, rather than individual pleasure, and that wickedness is more brutish than human. Goodness, he claimed, never fails to receive its appropriate reward, which is lost only when one stops being good. Boethius inaugurated the seven-fold medieval course of "liberal arts" study, characteristic of later medieval universities: the "trivium" of grammar, logic, and rhetoric, and "quadrivium" of arithmetic, geometry, astronomy and music. His influence was great, extending to Dante (1265-1321) and Chaucer (1345-1400), and his world view helped to give unity to medieval Europe.

Characteristic of the scholastic hair-splitting in philosophical and ethical matters by the medieval thinkers are the tracts of Anselm of Canterbury (1033-1109). Three of his dialogues (here between teacher and student) have been translated and introduced by Jasper Hopkins and Herbert Richardson (*Anselm of Canterbury on Truth, Freedom and Evil,* Harper Torchbooks, New York, 1967, 196 pp). He held that something is "right" when it is as it "ought" to be. This notion of the "ought" in ethics became well developed in "normative" ethical theory. It seems that some inspired authority, as the Church, decides what "ought" to be. Then, we all "ought" to be obedient to that authority. Under this kind of pressure, the cardinal virtue of obedience to authority became tempered by prudence, since disobedience, or deviation from the "norm," would inevitably bring unpleasant punishment. The orthodoxy was kept free from heresy by removing the heretics, although the Church hypocritically absolved itself from wrong or guilt by turning the heretics over to the "secular arm." Then, to compound the hypocrisy, in order to avoid the shedding of blood, which was admitted to be wrong, the heretics were burned. Yet, Anselm of Canterbury appears to have been a forthright honest intellectual, prejudiced toward Augustinian teachings, and by his argumentative skill justly called "the father of scholasticism." His efforts helped to further the notion that "sin" itself is a crime against society, and should be controlled by police suppression as well as by religious exhortation. This difficulty still haunts us, as illustrated by Charles McCabe, who, as a "fearless reporter", often calls attention to the difficulties we make for ourselves in trying to legislate morals. One might think we would learn our lesson from the evils brought upon us by the Prohibition Amendment of 1918-1933 to our Constitution.

The greatest writer on ethics in Christian medieval Europe, indeed its greatest philosopher, was Thomas Aquinas (1226-1274), the keen Italian friar in the Dominican order, who taught Aristotelianism at Paris, Rome, and Bologna. Knowing Aristotle only in Latin translation, and most of that from Arabic renderings of the original Greek, Aquinas nevertheless took him as his model, rather than Plato, and forged the *Summa Theologica,* a complete theological system harmonizing the knowledge of his time with the authoritative beliefs of the Church. This remains the standard authority in the Roman Church.

A convenient compendium is *The Pocket Aquinas* (Washington Square Press, New York, 1960, 372 pp.). with translations and introductions by Vernon J. Bourke. Aquinas made an *Exposition of the Nicomachean Ethics* of Aristotle, but his moral principles are found in all his writings. His ethic was theologically oriented, and was practiced in regard to purpose: "we live to attain happiness, and, in the world to come, everlasting contemplation of the "Perfect Good." He emphasized purposes, goals, and ends to be achieved, with realization that difficulty lies in the "prudent" selection and use of the means to gain those ends. Thus Prudence tends to supplant Obedience as the first of the cardinal Virtues, and the general position tends to the notion that the ends may justify the means. Here was the basis for the notorious Inquisition: in order to preserve the unity of faith, heresy must be sought out and destroyed. When heretics were burned, a priest was always in attendance to pray for the salvation of their souls!

Yet, Aquinas' moral principles were usually generalizations with apt examples. He said that there are ultimate standards of right and wrong, but that practical reason must start from the proposition that good should be done and evil avoided. Specifications for right and wrong actions develop in reasoning about specific actions. In general Aquinas takes the socially idealistic position of Plato that good actions are those contributing to the public and common welfare, and the Aristotelean compromise with hedonism in the perfection of oneself by understanding and self-control. Other actions or "habits" may be selfish, brutish, harmful to others or to oneself, and thus evil. In discussing differences between good and bad actions, Aquinas goes into detailed and lengthy reasoning, from which specific precepts of "natural moral law" emerge as conclusions.

Aquinas was not much concerned about one's individual moral problems, but was interested in general ethical principles. One's own moral problems were to him a matter of reasoning, and thus of prudence. One may be taught moral principles, but prudence, like judgment, can only be acquired by personal experience. Yet, in regard to fornication, Aquinas becomes quite specific in condemning as sinful any emission of semen "which takes place in a way whereby generation is impossible." He goes on to insist on the moral necessity for the proper rearing of offspring, even if born out of marriage. He concludes that "mariage is natural to humans, and an irregular connection outside of marriage is contrary to the good of humanity, and therefore fornication must be sinful." Aquinas would be expected to condemn abortion, and he does: "After the sin of murder, whereby the generation of human nature is precluded, seems to hold second place." Chastity is the implied sex morality of Aquinas.

The practical character of Thomistic teaching is indicated in Aquinas' discussion on the possession and use of material things. This is worth transcribing from Bourke's excellent translation of *Summa Theologiae* II-II, 66, 2:

> Two items are appropriate to people in reference to external things. One of these is the power to obtain and dispose of them. In regard to this it is proper for individual persons to possess things of their own. Indeed, it is even necessary for human life, for three reasons.
>
> The first reason is because individual people are more zealous in caring for something that belongs to them individually alone, than for something that is common to all or to a group, because every person avoids work and leaves to the other fellow whatever belongs to the community, as happens when there is a plurality of officials.
>
> The second reason is that human possessions are handled in a more orderly way, if it is incumbent on each one to provide his or her own things for themselves individually; there would be confusion if each person were to try to take care of everything without any division of labor.
>
> The third reason is because this system preserves the condition of mankind in a more peaceful way, provided that each person is satisfied with his or her own possessions. Consequently, we observe that among those who possess something in common and without any distinction of interest, quarrels frequently arise.
>
> Now the other item that is appropriate to people in regard to external things is the use of them. Concerning this, a person should not hold external things as his or her own, but as common; that is, in such a way that "one will share them with others in cases of need. Hence the Apostle says (I Tim.): Charge the rich of this world to give readily, sharing with others.

It would seem that, in this slightly ambiguous discussion, Aquinas is favoring not only private property, but also a modified communistic use of it.

In all medieval European ethical formulations there is always the overriding dark shadow of the concept of the Big Boss, the omniscient, omnipotent God, true or otherwise, in which all people believed, and with reference to which they behaved, either in fear of punishment or in hope of reward. This is well illustrated in Anne Freemantle's witty account *The Age of Belief: The Medieval Philosophers* (Mentor Books, New York, 1954, 218 pp). Most of medieval philosophical discussion revolved around the nature and quality of God. An important aspect of this was the major medieval philosophical problem of "universals," whether such concepts were real, or merely semantic symbols, as claimed by Abelard (1079-1142), the romantic Parisian lover of Heloise. Aquinas induced universal concepts from singulars.

During the long thousand years of medieval Europe from the fall of Rome in the 5th Century to the fall of Constantinople in the 15th, there were developing ethical formulations among the Muslims. The same sort of philosophical problems were discussed by them as among the Christians. Indeed, Averrhoes (1126-1198) of Cordoba, was known, even among the Christians, as the "Expositer of Aristotle." He taught the existence of a Universal Reason, shared in by all, which permits us all to communicate rationally. Interestingly, and almost alone, he denied the immortality of individuals but recognized the immortality of the human species. This has a modern ring, but then, Averrhoes was a physician and was practically oriented.

Other Muslim physicians were respected as philosophers, such as Rhazes (860-923) of Persia, and Avicenna (980-1037), also of Persia. Both wrote practical moral precepts, especially in relation to personal hygiene. Rhazes disapproved of the formulized Jewish, Christian and Islamic religions, all of which he thought have brought more evil than good, and each of which is self-contradictory. Avicenna's philosophical ideas influenced Aquinas. The most influential of Muslim ethical thinkers, however, was Moses Maimonides (1135-1204), a converted Jew from Cordoba who became physician to the great and magnanimous Saladin (1137-1193), Sultan of Syria and Egypt. Saladin's chivalry, good faith, piety and justice were recognized even by his chief opponents in the Crusades, which captured so much of the Syrian coast. These qualities are those recommended by Maimonides. In his *Guide for the Perplexed,* Moses Maimonides tried to compromise the wisdom of the Old Testament with that of Aristotle. His moral maxims were practical and probably inspired by his experience as a physician.

As summed up by Bertrand Russell (*A History of Western Philosophy,* Simon & Schuster, New York, 1945, 895 pp.),

> Throughout the Middle Ages, the Mohammedans were more civilized and more humane than the Christians. Christians persecuted Jews, especially at times of religious excitement; the Crusades were associated with appalling pogroms. In Mohamammedan countries, on the other hand, Jews were not in any way ill treated. Especially in Moorish Spain, they contributed to learning.

However, in both the Christian and Muslim cultures, the Zoroastrian identification of women with darkness and evil, and of men with light and goodness, persisted. The monastic ethic of submissiveness fostered the inferior;status of women, in spite of the growing worship of the Virgin Mary and the rise of the concept of chivalry. Since this ethic extolled submissiveness, it gave an opportunity for aggressiveness and dominance to those strong-willed enough to take it.

The climax of the Middle Ages in Europe came in the 13th Century, sometimes called "greatest of centuries." At this time all the peoples of Europe had a unity of belief and of behavior which expressed itself in yearning for the highest. This was exemplified in the aspiring upward-pointing of the great Gothic cathedrals. These must have been inspiring and morally awesome to all who worshipped sincerely in them, even as today they excite the admiration of tourists. But changes were coming. The Crusades opened the eyes of Europeans to the splendors of Muslim culture. Trade opened up, and with it new forces entered the European scene.

The Ethic of Enjoyment of Living
The Renaissance Ethic: Scepticism and Humanism

As Giorgio de Santillana says (*The Age of Adventure,* Mentor Books, New York, 1956, 283 pp.), in comparison with the long thousand years of the Age of Belief, the Renaissance was like an explosion. Trade fostered exchange of ideas; printing supplanted handcopying; the Americas were discovered; the world was "encompassed," the macrocosm of the universe expanded and our world was no longer its center; the microcosm of any human yielded to precise description, and delineation of religious dogma was challenged, and even as the new scientific endeavor displaced the magic of ages, the humanism of poetry, literature, music and the visual arts began to flourish. Moral repressions were loosened, and people began to enjoy living, or to try to do so.

The Renaissance began with the exchange of ideas in trading centers. One of the most important for trade between the eastern and western Mediterranean was at Salerno, on the southwest coast of Italy, below Vesuvius. Here a hospital must have been provided for the sick or injured seamen. There were so many that quite a group of physicians and surgeons were in attendance. Their skill was great enough to attract students to work with them. They needed books for reference, and these were easily brought by the traders from the east. But since they were in Arabic (the general Muslim language) they had to be translated into Latin (the general Christian language).

Some of the original Greek texts were brought also, such as those of Plato, Aristotle, Hippocrates and Galen. Greek had practically disappeared as a cultural language, except in Irish monasteries. Scholars had to learn to read it, and to render it into Latin. They found discrepancies between translations into Latin of Greek and Arabic versions of the same material. Thus textual criticism began, and it gradually became apparent that editorial manipulation might result in questioning of even supposedly "sacred" writings. Scepticism of authority was a Renaissance characteristic. It could arise at Salerno, where the school was not associated in any way with the Church.

This was not the case with the Universities which gradually arose in many centers such as Bologna (1158), Paris (1110), Oxford (1167), Cambridge (1209), Padua (1222), Salamanca (1243), Montpelier (1181) and even Prague (1348). These remained the strongholds of traditional conservatism, with their four faculties of Theology, Law, Medicine, and Liberal Arts. In these universities moral philosophy was dominated by Church dogma, supported by rationalizations based on Aristotle and Aquinas. Such scepticism as came from study and comparison of Greek, Arabic and Hebraic texts was smothered in scholastic trivia. Yet, the newly awakened interest in the excitement of living brought the intellectual rebirth, which soon flourished in open debate and which led to the "Reformation," and its resulting bitterness.

Characteristic thinkers of the general Renaissance who influenced the growth of ethical theory were Leonardo da Vinci (1452-1519), Desiderius Erasmus (1466-1536), and Francois Rabelais (1494-1553). Their impact was mainly on the broad front of emphasizing the worth, to individuals and humanity in general, of the "truth" about ourselves and our environment. Precision and exactness of knowledge was sought by them, with rare psychological insight in regard to the applications of knowledge about ourselves to human welfare in general. Erasmus wrote a widely circulated humanisticly cheerful essay (*Enconium Morial,* 1509) *"The Praise of Folly,"* (University of Michigan Press, 1958, 150 pp., in the

1668 English translation of John Wilson), and Rabelais wrote his witty and wise *Pantagruel* (1532) and *Gargantua* (1534), not merely to help sick people get well by laughing, but also, in satirizing conditions of the time, to stress the necessity of common sense in meeting the problems of every day.

Leonardo da Vinci is, and was in his own day, the prime example of the extraordinary success, in spite of his own frustrations, of the intellectual union of scientific endeavor, technology, and artistic enterprise. His great moral influence was exerted more by example than by precept. His writings and notebooks are only now in our time being fully appreciated. His artistic achievements commanded awe in his own day, in spite of the greater quantitative accomplishment of his chief rival, Michelangelo Buonarotti (1475-1564). His own notes, as well as his busy life reflect his joy in living, his abounding curiosity about the physical and psychological make-up of people, and about the thrilling mysteries of the world about us. His rationalism, untutored though he was, was a tremendous force against prevailing superstition and irrationalism, and his ethical position was one of unbiased regard for the welfare of living things, including people. Yet, he could and did invent, or foresee, terrible weapons for warfare. It was this apparent inconsistency which so greatly troubled his pupils, as discussed so well by Leonardo's most perceptive biographer, Dimitri Merezhkoski (1865-1941) in his *The Romance of Leonardo* (Modern Library, New York, 1928, 637 pp., translated by B. J. Guerney). This book gives as fine a picture of the intellectual and emotional turmoil of the Renaissance as can be found.

Gradually emerging in the Renaissance was the objective and rational search for the "truth" about ourselves and our environment, upon which a rational ethic can be built. It is remarkable that the two revolutionary books, which inaugurated the new era of scientific enterprise should have appeared in the same year, 1543, both from physicians: the *De Revolutionibus* of Nicolas Copernicus (1473-1543), which opened the new approach to the macrocrosm of the universe and the *De Fabrica Humani Corporis* of Andreas Vesalius

WHAT ARE WE LIVING FOR?

(1514-1564), which delineated the microccosm of the structure of human bodies. With these two books, scientific endeavor was well under way, with resulting huge repercussions in ethical theory.

Machiavelli and the Ethic of Power at Any (Reasonable?) Price

One of Leonard's Florentine contemporaries was Nicolo Machiavelli (1469-1527), a brilliant but sour writer, who frankly argued that deceit and wrong doing by a ruler are justified by the wickedness and treachery of the governed. Although he was much of a local historian, and even dramatist, Machiavelli's fame, or notoriety, is based chiefly in his seemingly cynical *Il Principe,* published in Rome in 1532. It is available in English by Luigi Ricci (Mentor Books, New York, 1952, 127 pp., introduction Christian Gauss), and by George Bull (Penguin Books, Baltimore, 1961, 154 pp.).

Deeply imbued with patriotic ardor for an Italy free from foreign domination, Machiavelli was convinced that a strong native government, even though absolute and tyranical, must be endured. For the establishment and maintenance of such an authoritarian government, he condoned any means. This extreme position, taken by totalitarian governments in our own time, was condemned as "devilish" in both France and England, and Mephistophelian deceit became synonymous with Machiavellianism. As Bull says, it became "as acceptable to call the Devil Machiavellian as it was to call Machiavelli diabolical." Machiavelli became a scapegoat for religious controversialists. Although he never attacked Church dogma, he was scathingly anticlerical and bitterly exposed the corruption of the Borgian papacy. On the other hand, as tutor of Catholic kings, he was condemned by the anti-Catholic factions as being responsible for their excesses. Unsuccessful as a diplomat or governmental officer, Machiavelli put his ideas into print, and thus they had more lasting influence than the example of his rather disappointing life.

While *The Prince* is mainly a treatise on the art of government, its influence on moral theory and practice was great, for it justified the ruthless imposition of power over others, on the part of those arrogant and often cruel enough to seize it, by whatever means. Since success and power were held in high social esteem in Machiavelli's time, as ours, his answer to the question of what one is living for, is simply to obtain and to exploit socially approved goals, "to get away with it," by fair means or foul. Essentially, it is an ethic of "might makes right," a principle followed by aggressive land hungry people from remote antiquity. It is related to the "Big Boss" principle which each child learns. It is a cynical ethic, and yet there is a modicum of decency in it, in that socially approved goals, even though they may foster individual success and power, imply some degree of concern for social welfare. The recent activities of Howard Hughes afford a remarkable example of current Machiavellicism. And the history of any authoritarian state, whether Nazi, fascist, communistic or even democratic, carries the generally repugnant smell of Machiavelli.

The Reformation and the Puritan Ethic

The scandalous excesses of the Borgian papacy in the early 16th century, with the growing hypocrisy of the venal selling of "indulgences" (fees or bribes for ecclesiastical pardon of "sins") led to an inevitable reaction. It began quietly but effectively when the Augustinian professor of theology at the South German University of Wittenberg, Martin Luther, (1483-1536) tacked 95 "theses" to the door of the Wittenberg cathedral on November 1, 1517. Those spelled out his preaching against indulgences and papal corruption. Students flocked to hear. Church finances were threatened as sale of indulgences declined, and every effort was made to silence Luther. But the people were with him.

Luther's was a practical ethic of self-control, self-understanding, and self-interpretation of sacred writing. It was a puritannical ethic, appreciated by common people, but directed toward community and social welfare as well as toward individual self-confidence. Although from peasant stock, Luther was scholar enough to translate the Bible into German vernacular, as well as musician and poet enough to compose solid devotional hymns, and vigorous enough to write many carefully argued treatises. Among these were *Assertions,* in which he denied free will on the part of anybody.

Erasmus defended free will in his *Diatribe* (Basle, 1524), and to this Luther replied in another vehement denial of free will, *De Servo* (1525). These are translated and edited by Ernst F. Winter (*Erasmus-Luther: Discourse on Free Will,* Fr. Ungar, New York, 1961, 138 pp.). Erasmus saw Christianity as a moral guide to simplicity of life and thought. Luther abhorred the Renaissance humanism, and was too serious for tolerance. He wanted to establish for all people what he thought was the truth, regardless of consequence. Thus, the effort of Erasmus at rational and ethical means for reform failed, and the Reformation spawned the Counter-Reformation. With escalating emotions, violence was inevitable, and fed horribly on itself.

More humanistically oriented than Luther was John Calvin (1509-1564) who prudently left France for Geneva where he founded the University, and preached salvation by faith. His zealous necessity for defending the faith, as he saw it, led him to condemn Miguel Servetus, the Spanish physician, to the stake for the revival of the Arian heresy implied in the strange volume *Restitutio Christianismi* (1553), all but three copies of which burned with the author. In this book Servetus gives the first full account of the pulmonary blood circulation, putting him among the medical greats. This description occurs in a discussion on the anatomical site of the "soul." Servetus had fled to Geneva, hoping for refuge, after the appearance of his earlier work, *De Erroribus Trinitatis,* obviously heretical. As a rational preacher and writer, Calvin did much to set the course of the rising Protestantism in Europe with his great Latin treatise of 1534 on the *Institutes of the Christian Religion.* Unfortunately, this tended toward a codification of rules for decent and theologically acceptable conduct instead of considering broad ethical principles.

Even more rigorous in puritannical mores was the Scot peasant, John Knox (1505-1572), who nevertheless learned

Greek and Hebrew at St. Andrews. He wrote against the evil
inherent in women in a characteristic patriarchal manner, and
yet he preached universal cooperation among people. Insisting
on the freedom of one's individual conscience, he nonetheless
made strict "covenants" with his followers in regard to
puritannical standards of life.

The net result of the 16th Century reformers was a return to
the Pauline patriarchal puritannical ethic, particularly emphasizing the inherent evil of sexual activity for purposes other
than procreation. An extraordinary disease phenomenon may
have had much to do with this position. In 1493, after the
second voyage of Columbus to the New World, a devastating
epidemic of a venereal disease broke out in Western Europe. It
was popularly thought to have been brought to Europe by the
sailors of Columbus. However, as soon as it appeared, the
most effective remedy, inunction by mercurial ointment, was
used. This had probably been introduced by the Muslims as
early as the 11th Century, for treatment of the "large pox."
Yet, the new epidemic was serious, whether due to a new
infectious organism or to a recrudescence of virulence in one
to which immunity had been lost. It was called variously by the
terms, "Spanish pox," the Italian "disorder" or the "French
disease" by people anxious to put the blame for it on their
neighbors. A humanistic and skilled physician of Verona,
Girolamo Fracastoro (1483-1553), wrote a remarkable poem
about the disease, *Syphilis, sive morbo gallicus* (Verona,
1530), in which the career of the hero of the poem, Syphillis, is
used as a background to discuss the etiology, symptoms,
diagnosis, prognosis and treatment. So successful was this
poem (it ran into many editions and translations) that the
name of the hero became the name of the disease. Certainly
the disease was considered by the puritans as a proper
punishment for carnal sin.

Another aspect of the "purity of thought" movement of the
European Reformation was the extraordinary interest in and
fear of witchcraft. H. R. Trevor-Roper has made a careful
survey of the extensive ramifications of this phenomenon, with
its resulting heresy hunts in Germany and Spain (*The European Witch-Craze of the 16th and 17th Centuries,* Harper,

New York, 1969, 246 pp.) He details how the Dominican order of preachers pressured the Roman Church into establishing the notorious Inquisition, with all its sadistic torture apparatus, for the purpose of stamping out doctrinal dissent, and keeping the faith pure. It moved especially against alleged witches, often merely illiterate emotionally motivated women, and Jews. Thousands perished in flames or by hanging. Torture was justified on the grounds that only under severe pain would a "ture" answer be given that was sought in the question put by the inquisitor.

The witch mania was widespread, even fouling the English colonies in North America, as exemplified in the Salem witch trials. This was the English puritanical reflection of the orthodox Roman Church's Inquisition. This latter was largely the result of the efforts of the Dominicans, founded about 1216 by Dominic Guzman (1170-1221) of Castile. The persistence of the witch cult, essentially a matriarchal carry-over of animistic and erotic ritual and belief, has been well discussed by Robert Graves (1896-   ) in his amazingly erudite but undocumented *The White Goddess* (Faber, London, 1948, 3rd Ed., 1959, 496 pp.). Popularly it is still reflected in opera and literature in descriptions of the "Witches' Sabbath" or Walpurgis Night.

Astonishingly there is current revival of various aspects of demonology, astrology, and witchcraft among our rebellious hippies and counter-culturists. Its erotic character is well exemplified in the plausible irrationality of *The Satanic Bible* (Avon, New York, 1969, 272 pp.) by the circus showman, Anton Szandor LeVey. It is a current version of ancient African voodoo, of the Hell-Fire Club of 18th Century England, of the Satanic Circle of Aleister Crowley in the 19th Century England, and the Black Order of Germany flourishing after World War I.

The Renaissance and Reformation were profound social revolutions in European culture. They opened many new and exciting vistas for exploration, both physically and intellectually. Yet many of the staid traditional ways of thinking and behaving persisted. New freedoms for ethical consideration brought a sobering sense of responsibility. Those in authority often abused it cruelly. It is to be remembered, however, that a universal belief in immortality gave a convenient excuse that a higher final justice would prevail in an after-life. Even the members of the then Establishment could shudder with common people at the solemn warning in the *Requiem,*

> Mors stupebit e natura
> Cum resurget creatura
> Judicanti responsura,

Death and Nature shall be amazed, when all creation rises again to answer to the Judge. The solemn but quite irrational *Requiem* has inspired our greatest musical composers, perhaps none to surpass Hector Berlioz (1803-1869) in his *Grande Messe des Morts* (1837), which continues to tax our finest endeavor.

The New Ethics of Rationalism

The late Renaissance ushered in a new rationalistic approach to ourselves and our environment. New information about the world and what's in it came as a flood. It was rapidly spread by printing, and it provoked thought, wonder, action and reaction, as in the Reformation and Counter-Reformation. In all the emotional storm and fury, however, there were a few calm, quiet voices, speaking gently, and often wittily for tolerance. Such a voice was that of Erasmus. Another was that of Michel Esquem de Montaigne (1533-1592), Mayor of Bordeaux, lover of good wines, and charming essayist.

Montaigne added little to ethical theory in a direct way. But in his haphazard critique of the exciting life of his time there are many indications of a growing moral rationalism. Essentially a sceptic, Montaigne gave a clear example of tolerant willingness to learn and to understand, even divergent or conflicting views. He held that to be sincere and truthful is the beginning of virtue. Generalizations are treacherous, he realized, so he taught that it is wise not to expect much of anybody or anything, in order to avoid disappointment. Sincere friendship he considered to be a real blessing. Montaigne's tolerant and sceptical position prepared the way for the growing rationalism of the 17th Century.

The great counter-culture of the vigorous youngsters of the 17th Century in Western Europe was all for the new science and against the old traditional speculative wishful thinking often burdened with a superstitious load of magical and emotional belief. It was the result of the clar demonstration, usually by experiment, of the ways our bodies work, and of the manner in which our environment acts.

Copernicus (1473-1543), Tycho Brahe (1546-1601), Kepler (1541-1630), and Galileo (1564-1642) had put the universe in a rational frame and had demonstrated some of the principles of how it and our world is put together. The "how" of things became much more interesting than the "why." Vesalius (1514-1564), and William Harvey (1578-1651), showed how our bodies are put together, and how they work. While the astronomers revealed how powerful mathematics is for solid reasoning, Harvey laid the foundation for "natural science" on the sequence of (1) careful observation and accurate reporting of a phenomenon; (2) a tentative explanation of it; (3) a direct testing of the proposed explanation (hypothesis) by experiment, with quantitative measurement of whatever variables in the experiment are thus controllable and (4) conclusions drawn from the results of the experiments.

This method of Harvey, first displayed in his little 72 page classic, *De Motu Cordis* (Frankfurt, 1628), in which he demonstrated the circulation of the blood, provided the power for modern science. It showed how agreement could be reached by independent verification of the conclusions, if unbiased repetition of the experiment would give the same figures. This introduced an entirely new, but most powerful method of getting the truth about ourselves and our environment. Harvey probably learned quantitative experiments from Galileo, who was teaching at Padua when Harvey studied medicine there.

One consequence of the detailed discussion of specific moral duties as made by Thomas Aquinas in *Summa Theologiae* was a growing pedantry in definitiona and distinction. Thomas showed sober judgment with moral standards, but his petty scholastic followers buried it under legalism and casuistry. Manuals of morality, similar to catechisms appeared. Detailed scrutiny of cases resulted in widely differing opinions. As is characteristic of all detailed codes of conduct, the more effort spent in deducing conclusions, where the distinction between what is allowable and what is prohibited, the greater the disagreement among the teachers. During and after the Reformation, the Catholic Church, in order to recover its hold on people, had to champion the principle of social authority against reliance on private individual judgment.

In support of this, the Jesuits, with psychological insight, sought to make the confessional attractive, accommodating ecclesiastical moral law to the reality of common worldly needs as felt by ordinary people. This resulted in the ethical theory of "probabilism," by which any probable opinion of some recognized thinker could be used to justify action. It was considered to be the duty of a confessor to propose such an opinion if it would relieve the depressing burden of the conscience of an individual confessing some wrong doing. Here was a practical recognition of the psychological impossibility of a moral generality, or absolute, appealing with equal force to all people. The Jesuits, founded in 1534 by Ignatius de Loyola (1491-1556), a zealous religious enthusiast, have ever tempered their logical rigor by a wise psychological insight. Thus they have been extremely successful in upholding the highest intellectual standards of the Catholic Church. Their practical wisdom is reflected in their recognition of what we call "conditioning," in their saying, "Give us the children until they are seven years, and they will always be ours." This psychological wisdom was known to and practiced by the Chinese. Its modern analysis will ever be associated with Ivan Pavlov (1849-1936), in his famed studies in "conditional reflexes."

As shown so well by Henry Sidgwick (1839-1900), the liberal Cambridge intuitionist, in his historical account of ethical theories (*Encyclopedia Brit.,* 11th Ed., Cambridge, 1911, Vol. X, pp. 810-840), the humanistic reaction of European thinkers in the 16th Century gave stimulus to the growth of a moral philosophy independent of either Catholic or Protestant assumptions. Thus Hugo Grotius (1585-1645) emphasized "natural law" as the basis for the desire of people to have tranquil associations with their fellows. A "state of nature" was postulated in which individuals and families lived side-by-side in peace, with no interpersonal injury, where all would have free use of the goods of the earth common to all, with respect for parental authority, fidelity in marriage, and the observance of compacts freely made. Grotius expanded this concept to international relations. Here general observance of "natural law" was especially important in regard to compacts or treaties. Grotius led to Hobbes.

The new scientific spirit enthused the young people of the 17th Century. They realized the dangers of bucking the Establishment: Giordano Bruno (1548-1600) was burned at the stake for his vigorous anti-Aristotelianism, and Galileo was harassed by the Inquisition. Yet, they pushed ahead with their rationalistic empiricism and soon had strong moral support. Two of the greatest thinkers of the time put the weight of their prestige and writings behind the growing rationalism, Thomas Hobbes (1588-1679), the English lawyer, and René Descartes (1596-1650), the French philosopher. Both insisted on the supremacy of reason over the emotions, and with cogent ethical consequences.

Hobbes strongly opposed scholasticism and its pedantry, and, traveling widely in the Continent as tutor to young noblemen, became well acquainted with the new rationalism. Distressed by the civil disorders of his time, Hobbes wrote *The Elements of Law* (1640) in which he defined a king's prerogatives on psychological grounds rather than on the spurious basis of "Divine Right." Impressed by mathematical and geometrical order, he wondered how similar order could be brought among people. He held that "good" and "evil" are inconstant terms applied almost haphazardly by people to what attracts or repels them.

Hobbes' masterpiece was *Leviathan* (London, 1651), readily available with a valuable introduction by C. B. MacPherson (Penguin Books, Baltimore, 1968, 729 pp.). In this he gave a rational basis for obedience to whatever civil authority actually excercised power at the time, in order to obtain the benefits of social order. He showed how egoism produces nastiness and brutishness, with each person at odds with everyone else, and how rational, considered self-interest can guide us to surrender aggressive tendencies, but not self-defense, to the sovereignty of law, with freedom in what is not covered by law. This sovereign power is effective, said Hobbes, only as long as it can be enforced, and it makes no difference whether or not it is vested in a person or an assembly. He was condemned as an atheist, but was protected at the Restoration in England by Charles II. His ethical position was rationally directed toward social order from which each individual benefits.

René Descartes was a brilliant general scientist: he brought algebra and geometry together in his neat quantitative graphic device of correlating variables; he popularized Harvey's physiological work; he analyzed reflex nervous action and the physical principles of vision; and he developed a strong dualistic philosophy, in which the moral implication was that we'd all tend to get along with each other if we could use our reason to control our emotions. The dualism, however, was unfortunate, in that it assumed as much of a reality to the "mind" as to the "body." Yet, Descartes started the long study of the functioning of the human nervous system, including our brains, which only now is beginning to demonstrate what does, in fact, determine our mood and behavior.

Descartes' philosophical writings are large, complex, generally sceptical, and theological. This all seems to reflect his training as a Jesuit. Readily available are the English translations by Elizabeth Haldane and G. R. T. Ross (*The Philosophical Works of Descartes,* 2 volumes, Cambridge University Press, 1969, 452 - 380 pp.). His famed 2 Discourse on Method first appeated in Leyden in 1637, but his earliest essay was on *"Rules for the Direction of Our Intelligence"* in 1628, but not published until after his death. Actually Descartes did not specifically write on ethics or morals, but his ethical position may be inferred from his argument. It seems to be generally assumed that our emotions tend to lead us astray, and that our reason, or intelligence, should be used, if we wish to enjoy life, to control our emotions.

The Ethic of Law and Order

Descartes' effort was extended by Blaise Pascal (1623-1662) in exposing the emotional basis of despair, uncertainty, and guilt. He emphasized the dignity and power of reason, claiming again that in self-knowledge lies the greatness of humanity Descartes' work was further extended by Baruch Spinoza (1632-1677), the famed Jewish thinker expelled from his Amsterdam synagogue because of his interest in the new sciences of optics and astronomy. His *Ethica* appeared after his death. It is available in English translation by William H. White *(Ethics, and On the Improvement of the Understanding,* Hafner Publishing Co., New York, 1949, 260 pp.)

Spinoza, impressed with the growing realization of mathematical order in the universe thought that a similar order might be developed (or found) in human affairs. He tried to deduce moral principles as theorems derived from religious assumptions or axioms. Thus his ethical position tended toward an absolutism. His writing was organized along Euclidean demonstration lines, and while idealistic, it gives an impression of finality. But he espoused the new rationalism vigorously: to him wrong action is synonymous with rational error. Thus he allied the logics to the ethics.

A similar mathematical absolutism was propounded by Gottfried Wilhelm Leibniz (1646-1716). The new scientific discoveries about order in the universe, especially as developed by Isaac Newton (1642-1727), profoundly affected moral and political theory. If mathematical law and order is to be found in the universe, as so well demonstrated by Newton, then it should similarly exist among people. So went the subconscious argument. And as the mathematical law and order in the universe is absolute, fixed and final, so must it be among people. This point of view was behind the works of Spinoza and Leibniz, and after Newton, it dominated Immanuel Kant (1724-1804). These men were all astronomers and mathematicians, and mathematical orderliness was characteristic of their thought.

So there came an absolutism in ethical theory, and in politics as well. In political theory, however, especially in the English speaking world, the practical problems of effective government tended toward democratic principles, thanks largely to John Locke (1632-1704). Yet, the constitution of the United States of America (1789) was essentially a Newtonian document, with its checks and balances, and the absolutism of it as the "law of the land."

It is difficult to capsulate Kant's ethical theory. It assumed, it seems, an absolute right or goodness, the seeking of which was a "categorical imperative" for each of us to undertake. Similar to the "innate" concepts of time and space, which, he said, are part of the structures of our "minds," this "categorical imperative" is also part of the way in which our minds work.

Practically, this idea was no more successful than it was in theory. After much turgid language, Kant sets out as a practical guide to conduct that we should always so act as if our action could become a universal way of acting. This is clearly an absolutist ethic, quite impossible for any one to follow under the ordinary stresses and strains of living. It assumes an intelligence so far denied to us mortals, but it does focus attention on the consequences of conduct. Yet, it seems to ignore the obvious psychological differences between us: some of us remain oriented toward social welfare, some of us toward our own personal pleasures, and some of us toward power at any cost.

Kant was an astronomer, full of the wonder and mystery of the universe, but not as well aware of the mystery of differing personalities. Kant must have thought of people as fixed, as immutable and as subject to mathematical orderliness as the stars. His emphasis on "duty" suggests that he may have thought this to be the essential driving force to orderliness among people, even as gravity is among the stars. Several

English translations of Kant's ethical writings are available; one of the most helpful is H.J. Paton's translation and analysis of *Groundwork of the Metaphysic of Morals* (Harper & Row, New York, 1964, 148 pp.).

The Empirical Ethic of Experience

Meanwhile a more practical down-to-earth approach to the problem of living had been developed by John Locke (1632-1704), the rationalizing physician who was such a close friend of the great theory-spurning physician, Thomas Sydenham (1624-1689). It was Sydenham's empirical success in treating fevers by the "Bark" (Cinchona bark, brought from Peru, by the Spaniards), with complete disregard for the long traditional humoral theory of disease, which had great influence on the rise of English empiricism. Locke based his moral principles on experience, even as his general philosophy taught that it is the experience of living, writing as it were on the initially blank tablet of the brain, which determines our various ways of thinking.

Locke was thus a pioneering psychologist. His insights led him to seek methods by which people could come to agreements, a problem of perennial importance. Here he made a significant advance in the theory of democratic action over the ancient Athenian town-meeting procedure. Locke pointed out that if the people of a community have access to the same body of "sound" (he probably meant "verifiable") information they are more likely to come to reasonable agreement on matters of public policy than would be the case if they did not.

Locke's principles had much influence on the development of democratic principles in the USA. Thus, Benjamin Franklin (1706-1790), our remarkable scientist-humanist, advocated free public libraries for the purpose of providing the people of a community with access to the same body of "sound" information, in order to aid in reaching agreements on public policy. Similarly, Thomas Jefferson (1743-1826), our keen statesman-technologist-humanist, proposed free public schools, so that people in a community might have the background of the same "sound" information for the formulation of agreeable public policies.

We could further extend Locke's principle, and for a much wider community: those public institutions such as universities, or research institutes, which generate such an abundance of new "sound" information might well arrange to send this information about ourselves and our environments freely to other public institutions all over the world. To be useful, this vast accumulation of essentially scientific information must be analyzed and condensed, with synthesis of emerging generalities, into books and reviews brief enough to be readily comprehended. In this effort computer technology is already aiding. In order, however, to be really effective in Locke's sense of helping us to reach agreements on social and public policy, it must be *freely* available to all who are competent to use it, in all parts of the world. This will require wide governmental support, and probably could be handled most satisfactorily by the United Nations, if our various governments would cooperate. In a small way this was tried in the quarterly publication, *Texas Reports on Biology and Medicine* (started in 1943) which does go without cost to the libraries of biomedical institutions all over the world.

A pupil of John Locke was Anthony Ashley Cooper, Third Earl of Shaftesbury (1671-1713). He modified Locke's position by postulating a "moral sense" or ethical intuition, independent of reason. He tried to show the innate naturalness of our social gregariousness and the experience of harmonizing this with our individual self-regarding impulses. His idea was that individual people are part of a larger system (a society), so that "goodness" is what contributes to the welfare of the whole, and thus also is conducive to the happiness of the individual. His *Characteristics of Men, Manners, Opinions, Times* (1711) made psychological experience the basis of a harmony ethic.

A typical English 18th Century divine was Joseph Butler (1692-1752), who further developed the idea of morals being derived from psychological experience and intuition. In his *Fifteen Sermons* (1726), he outlines his position that virtue is a balance between the psychological factors of the passions, of the reflective principles of self-love and benevolence, and of conscience. Another follower of Shaftesbury's intuitive psychology was Francis Hutcheson (1694-1746), the Glasgow proponent of common-sense. He also was influenced by Locke. His *System of Moral Philosophy* (1755) differentiated the relative calmness of benevolence from turbulent passions, and separated strictly ethical considerations from those referring to decency and dignity. He thus differentiated ethics from etiquette, a distinction the neglect of which often results in confusion, as in the case of the conduct of health professionals.

In concluding this discussion of the ethics of rationalism and experience, it seems that, in a way analogous to an individual, our species, during the exciting 17th Century, was growing up. People had been through a lot. Their early idealism had been tempered by the harsh realities of living. Many ways had been tried in the effort to answer that ever-present question of, *"What are we living for?"* Experience with plain facts of living were beginning to be effective. After Descartes and Locke, people were going to be increasingly guided by reason and experience. With the great increase of scientific effort, with its increasing verifiable knowledge about ourselves and our environment, we would seem increasingly able to get a satisfying answer to that perplexing question of, *"What are we living for?"*. We are continuing as a species to grow older, and even as an aging individual may grow in wisdom, so may we as a species.

The Ethic of Doubt

The 18th Century is often called *The Age of Enlightenment,* which Isaiah Berlin used as the title of the book he edited (Mentor Books, New York, 1956, 282 pp.). The industrial revolution was under way; people were moving from rural areas to factory towns with their squalid overcrowding; technology was exploiting scientific discoveries, and people generally were looking toward more material goods and toward self-government. Wide education and growing nationalism were fermenting the American and French Revolutions.

Yet doubts were arising. The cosmic optimism of Leibniz and its "all for the best in this best of all possible worlds," was laughed away by the wit of Francois Marie Voltaire (1694-1778) in his *Candide* (1759). Bishop George Berkeley (1685-1753), who worked awhile in Rhode Island, showed some of the semantic traps in the relation of words and symbols to things, and that ideas are formed by the imprint of the senses with the help of memory and imagination. He was critical of Locke, and his work in general cast doubt on the validity of moral terms. That ever ambivalent opportunist, Jean Jacques Rousseau (1712-1778), who extolled the innocence of children but placed his own in the Parisian Foundling Hospital, doubted that the arts and the now flourishing sciences could favorably influence morality. He won a prize in 1750 by asserting that the sciences degrade us from our naturally noble condition, and by creating artificial wants, decrease our freedom. His slogan, "Liberty, Equality, Fraternity," became the watchword of the French Revolution. But he died insane.

The greatest sceptic of the 18th Century was David Hume (1711-1776), pride of Edinburgh. He argued that perceptions in our minds are impressions of which we are immediately aware in experience, as sensations and emotions, and then ideas which are faint echoes of sensations and emotions arising when we think and try to reason. He denied any necessary connection between cause and effect, claiming that this notion of causation comes from our habit of associating certain events with others. Specifically in ethical theory, Hume exposed the "naturalistic fallacy," that is, the attempt to jump by deductive logic from what "is" to what "ought to be."

Hume insisted that it is more pertinent for us to understand what "is" in our world than to try to figure out what "ought to be." He was thus an existentialist. Indeed, he anticipated the 19th Century Romanticists by claiming that reason is the slave of the passions. In this he was an anti-rationalist, but a wise psychologist. He challenged the artificiality of the principles of justice and of moral obligation, or duty, and thus opposed the "natural law" theories of Hobbes, Locke, Kant and Rousseau. Hume's *Enquiry Concerning Human Understanding* (1748) provoked Kant. In 1751 appeared Hume's *Enquiry Concerning the Principles of Morals,* in which there was a start of a history of ethical theory. Hume was in fact an excellent historian, his six volumes *History of England* (1754-1762) making him famous abroad as well as at home. Magnanimously he tried to protect Rousseau in England, but the attempt failed. Hume was sceptical of conventional religion and of the Church. His *Natural History of Religion* offers a rationalistic account of the origin and growth of religious ideas, and questions the value of religious or theological influence on ethics, or on moral problems. This has been edited by H. E. Root (Stanford University Press, 1956, 76 pp.). Hume simply concludes that popular religions have a bad influence on morality.

The Ethic of Work: Methodism

The industrial revolution of the 18th Century in England brought many ills. The peace and simplicity of rural life was disrupted. The factories were grim places of weary and monotonous work. Hours of work were long, twelve a day and six days a week. Wages were low. Children were often cruelly exploited in the factories. Living accommodations in the crowded cities were often makeshift and generally appalling. Gin mills flourished, since cheap gin gave quick and drunken relief to the general misery. Food was expensive and malnutrition was widespread. Epidemics of infectious disease were frequent and smallpox was almost universal. Debtors' prisons were the end for many who became enslaved economically. Prostitution was prevalent, slums abounded, crime was common, and punishments were cruel. The nation kept some balance only by deporting debtors and criminals to the colonies - the Carolinas for economic slavery in the tobacco and cotton fields, and Australia for "good riddance." For the people it was the misery pictured for us by Hogarth.

Into this glum situation came two devoted brothers, John Wesley (1703-1791) and Charles Wesley (1707-1788). Both were educated at Christ Church, Oxford, and were ordained in the Church of England, showing remarkable conscientiousness and asceticism. They undertook a mission to Georgia as high churchmen, but had already formed a group of religious devotees called "Methodists" in derision. Experiencing a profound drive to correct the ills of the industrial revolution, to which the Church shut its eyes, the Wesleys boldly threw aside ecclesiastical tradition, and appealed directly to the masses in the open air. In 1739 the first Methodist chapel was built in Bristol. They got an old foundry in London, and soon thousands of working people would wait hours to hear them preach.

To the crowds of working people, miners, weavers, spinners, fishermen, day laborers, they preached the dignity of work and of people. They taught the worth of self-respect as a primary objective to be justified by faithful work and decent living.

Their answer to the eternal question of, *"What are we living for"*, was simple and direct: to earn our way with dignity, decency and self-respect. They preached against alcoholic beverages, tobacco, gambling, card playing, dancing, fornication, frivolity and licentiousness in any form. Their success was phenomenal. John preached some 40,000 sermons, and Charles wrote some 6500 hymns.

Preaching and singing hymns became the way of the sect, and they both gave a strong social unity to the movement. As a practical way of life, Methodism was a success, and it flourished in the Colonies as well as in England. It brought back a strict moral tone, puritannical but self-satisfying to the hard pressed people of the time, and it made it possible for them not only to survive, but to prosper. Their honesty, prudence, and hard work gave the followers of the Wesleys a social prestige that was justified, though it was humble, modest, and without ostentation.

Methodism was all embracing in its effort to bring dignity and self-respect to the masses. John Wesley wrote grammars, histories and biographies to aid his followers in self-education. He made collections of psalms and hymns. He wrote a popular medical compendium to help people treat their own ills and to prevent disease. He wrote manuals of gardening and nutrition, so that people could feed themselves. Although funds flooded in, he gave most to charity, founding orphans' homes, charity schools and dispensaries. In a very practical down-to-earth manner, John and Charles Wesley preached and practiced a wholesome ethic of good work with self-esteem and cheerful modesty.

A similar practical morality developed in the USA under the name of Mormonism. This resulted from the dreams of Joseph Smith (1805-1844), who was murdered by the envious neighbors of his followers in Illinois. In spite of a fling at polygamy and much irrational belief, Mormonism has flourished. This has resulted largely from the firm puritannical way in which they behave, from their purposeful work, their industriousness, and above all else, from their economic shrewdness, and scrupulous honesty in business. They have amazingly prospered in Utah. Their patriarchal ethos is solidly grounded in a work ethic. In this they well maintain their self-confidence and self-respect.

The Executive Ethic: Utilitarianism

Utilitarianism, a characteristic administrative ethic, is also characteristically English. It developed as a reaction of churchmen to the notion of Thomas Hobbes that the primeval natural state of humanity is one of anarchy and that civil organization is the source of all moral law. In 1672, Bishop Richard Cumberland (1631-1718) wrote *De Legibus Naturae,* in which he voiced the opinion of churchmen that the gospel of universal benevolence, which owes nothing to civil enactment, is both natural and conducive to happiness. Cumberland held that the greatest possible benevolence of every rational person toward everyone else constitutes the happiest state of each and all. He stressed the naturally social tendency of people, and thus that morality is a function of the social organism. Here is recognition of the importance of the differences in the biological organizational levels of people, as between individuals and societies.

Henry Stuart *(Encycl. Brit.,* 11th Ed., Cambridge 1911, Vol. 27, 820-822) considers that the ethical doctrine of utilitarianism went through three phases: (1) theological, inaugurated by Cumberland; (2) political, started by Jeremy Bentham (1748-1832) and (3) biological, as outlined by Charles Robert Darwin (1809-1882) in his *Descent of Man* (John Murray, London, 1871). This analysis makes utilitarianism a central item in the development of theories of ethics, and indeed much does revolve around it.

Theological utilitarianism was advanced in opposition to the idea that there is an innate moral sense, a subjective emotion, by which we approve benevolent action which may have no advantage to us. This moral sensitivity idea of Anthony Ashley Cooper Shaftesbury (1671-1713) and Francis Hutcheson (1694-1746) was well expressed in the latter's *Inquiry into the Original of Our Ideas of Beauty and Virtue* (Glasgow, 1720). It had something of Berkeley's subjectivity about it, but was discredited by William Paley (1743-1805) of Christ's College, Cambridge. His *Principles of Moral and Political Philosophy* (Cambridge, 1785) was common sense for his time, virtue consisting of doing good to all people, in obedience to the will of God, and for the sake of the lasting happiness of all.

Hume had already in his *Inquiry Concerning the Principles,* (Edinburgh, 1751) opted for utility in moral conduct, without religious overtones. He showed that the essence of benevolence is to increase the happiness of others. He said that personal merit consists in the "usefulness or agreeableness of qualities to the person possessed of them, or to others" in contact with that person. Hume defended a humanistic ethic, showing that morality is not a matter of subjective mysterious innate feelings, or abstract relations, or supernatural sanction, but depends on the current conditions of individual personal and social welfare.

Political utilitarianism developed with Jeremy Bentham (1748-1832) of London. Educated at Oxford, he became interested in the theory of law. He held that laws should be socially useful, and not merely reflect the *status quo.*People, he claimed, generally go after pleasure and avoid pain. Desires or drives he divided into self-regarding and other-regarding. The purpose of law, he said is to reward good behavior and to punish evil-doing, and to maintain justice. The principle of utility in ethics may have been succintly stated by Joseph Priestley (1733-1804), the liberal Birmingham clergyman and chemist who later settled in Pennsylvania, or even by Hutcheson or Hume. It was in the air of the times. It was the doctrine that the sole test of the goodness of moral precepts or of legislative enactments is their tendency to promote the greatest happiness for the greatest possible number of people.

In his secluded garden retreat in London, Bentham entertained friends, such as James Mill (1773-1836), with intellectual conversation. Utilitarianism was the name he gave to the moral principle of striving for the greatest good of the greatest

number, the characteristic ethic of administrators or executives. He prepared complex tables of motivation, and attempted to codify impulses, the needs of society, and institutions. His interest in private morals was merely to
appreciate those impulses necessary to be controlled by law, if
the social welfare were to be preserved. He sought to ask of all
institutions whether their utility would justify their existence.
Highly regarded in his long life,Bentham was embalmed at his
death, dressed as usual, and placed in his chair at University
College of which he was a patron.

Bentham's most effective follower as a utilitarian writer was
John Stuart Mill (1806-1873), the son of Betham's friend,
James. John was taught by his father, and like Bentham was a
precocious reader of Greek and Latin. He studied for a time at
Edinburgh, but soon took a place at India House, the
headquarters of the East India Company, which, though not a
government agency, did govern India with efficient skill until
it was dissolved in 1858. Mill married Harriet Hardy Taylor
in 1851, and she aided him in writing and in formulating his
ideas. The elder Mill and his wife were early women's libbers,
even to the point of deploring the use of "man" as the
designation for all humanity. Semantically this remains important: "man" provokes the image of a single male (often
old), whereas we really mean "people." The latter is not
merely more accurate, it also gives the plural referant which is
more correct when all humanity is meant. "People and their
future" is semantically preferable to "man and his future."
When the cliché'd latter is used, one might properly ask,
"which man?"

John Stuart Mill became the chief expositer of utilitarianism. His practicality was expressed in his many writings
on economic problems. Deploring the poverty and misery due
to economic factors, he sought equal distribution of the
products of labor, recognizing that while conditions of production are often set by physical circumstances, distribution of
produce is a matter of human arrangement. He sought
amelioration of hard working conditions, and plugged for
legislative representation of minorities. Much of this has a

current ring, but in Mill's case, it was probably an extension of the British aristrocratic sense of *noblesse oblige.* Yet, Mill seems to have had an apprehension of the potential tyranny of the majority in any group. This idea appeared in the penetrating *De la Démocratie en Amerique* (1835) of Alexis Clerel de Tocqueville (1805-1859), who, after a searching visit to the USA, concluded that greater equality requires greater concentration of government, and thus diminishes liberty. Mill emphasized the responsibility of executives to be fair to all, in promoting the greatest good for the greatest number.

Utilitarianism, as an ethical program, was well systematized by Mill. He classified pleasurable and painful sensations, endeavoring to develop a calculus of goodness and evil. It did not work out. He wished to avoid dogma, and showed much concern over the validity of evidence for various opinions. Tackling the problem of reaching agreement, he expanded Locke's ideas, taking his cue from the developing experimental science, especially in chemistry. He noted that the process of independent verification of an idea in scientific endeavor is what gives science its power and its validity. The agreement depends, he observed, that all involved use the same general methods of investigation, and have the same objective test of truth. Can this procedure of verification be followed in social affairs? Mill was pioneering in social sciences.

Mill appreciated that a satisfactory means of arriving at moral truth was not available. Yet he held that our intelligence is a more appropriate guide of morality than any sort of submission to authority. However, Mill included in his concept of utility the pleasures of imagination and the need for the gratification of emotional desires. After the dissolution of the East India Company, Mill retired to Avignon, where he botanized, and continued his writing. His essay on "Utilitarianism" appeared in *Fraser's Magazine* in 1861. Mary Warnock has edited some of Mill's characteristic essays, together with selections from Jeremy Bentham (Meridian Books, Cleveland, Ohio, 1965, 352 pp.).

Evolutionary Ethics: the Morality of Survival

The general notion of evolution had been floating about since the latter part of the 18th century. Erasmus Darwin (1731-1802), grandfather of the famed Charles, and also of the eugenicist, Francis Galton (1822-1911), had vague notions of evolutionary sequences among living things. But so had Aristotle. The evolutionary concept was first clearly outlined by Jean Baptiste Pierre de Monet, Chevalier de Lamarck (1744-1829). His *Philosophie Zoologique* (1809) gave his theories on the relations of species of animals, and on their origin, on the basis of functional adaptation. Even though he was primarily a botanist, he had broad interests in the whole scope of biology. He believed that characteristics of living things acquired in adapting to a particular environment could be passed along in an inherited manner. This concept became politically important in the USSR in the mid-20th Century, being a factor in the unfortunate dogmatism of Trofim Denisovich Lysenko (1898-   ). The problem is not yet satisfactorily solved.

The full force of the evolutionary theory of life, however, was revealed by the meticulous reports in *The Origin of Species by Natural Selection* (John Murray, London, 1859) by Charles Robert Darwin (1809-1882). This was based largely on the carefully detailed observations he had made while serving as naturalist on the long voyage (1831-1836) of H.M.S. Beagle in the South Pacific, including the isolated Galapagos Islands. Retiring to a country place in Down, Kent, he gradually formulated his thesis that species of living things arise by chance variations with survival favored by adaptation to the environment. His publication was precipitated by an essay submitted to him by Alfred Russell Wallace (1823-1913), working in the East Indies, who came to the same general conclusions.Magnanimously, Darwin reported Wallace's findings with his own to the Linnean Society of London, July 1, 1858, and then set to work on his notes in order to put his book in shape. It sold out promptly on its appearance and created a great stir in intellectual circles, since it was recognized at once to be a great threat to long established authoritarian tradition.

Darwin pushed his point in other books: *The Variation of Plants and Animals under Domestication* (1867) and notably, *The Descent of Man* (1871). In the latter, in which humans are shown to have an ancestry related to the higher apes, Darwin emphasized the importance of sexual selection in mammalian survival. He had vigorous support from the popularizations of Thomas Henry Huxley (1825-1895). The ethical implications of his great demonstration were well developed by Herbert Spencer (1820-1903), who had been thinking along evolutionary lines before *The Origin of Species* appeared in 1859.

Spencer's *Principles of Psychology,* developed along evolutionary lines, appeared in 1855. Darwin's *Origin of Species* was to Spencer a particular example of his own *à priori* ideas. Spencer was largely self-educated, and was early impressed with the progressive growth of ideas. He issued a large *System of Synthetic Philosophy* over a series of years, in which he argued that ultimate scientific principles are unknowable, but that this unknowable remains a power (call it "God") in the universe. Philosophy, he thought, could be a unifying factor in the sciences.

Spencer's *Principles of Ethics* appeared in parts; Part 1, *Data of Ethics,* in 1892; Part 2, *Induction of Ethics,* and Part 3, *Ethics of Individual Life,* also in 1892; Part 4, *Justice,* came first, in 1891 and Parts 5 and 6, *Negative and Positive Beneficences,* were published in 1893. It is clear that Spencer was an orderly and comprehensive thinker on moral problems, even though the chronology of his ethical writing was erratic. His general view of the evolutionary process was embodied in his phrase, "survival of the fittest," by which he implied a reciprocal relation between living things and their environment. This was echoed in 1913 by the provocative volume, *The Fitness of the Environment,* of Lawrence J. Henderson (1878-1942), the brilliant Harvard biochemist. The general idea of survival of that which fits remains much in the air, and has been extended, as we shall see, to living relationships as well as to living objects.

Spencer, in general, relies on scientific objectivity and the materialism of natural life. His was, in part, an attempt at a scientific ethic. Existentialists might criticize him for denying a place for subjective feeling in his system. They don't, however; they merely ignore him. Yet such a criticism would be unfair. He emphasizes that egoism is primal, since there must be egoistic pleasure before there can be altruistic sympathy with it. Further, one can get egoistic pleasure from altruistic acts. The notion of duty, thought Spencer, is an idea imposed on people by their religious and political superiors. The feeling of duty is a transitory one, giving way subjectively to self-moralizing.

Spencer emphasized the awareness of the consequences of behavior as a basis for guidance of conduct. Developing an evolutionary hedonism, he noted that there is a sort of pleasure in actions which are conducive to survival. He considered asceticism to be self-defeating, but that socially approved ("good?") conduct leads to the preservation of a pleasurable life in a society adjusted so that each member thereof attains happiness without impeding that of others therein. Life, he claims, is valuable in proportion to the extent to which it brings happiness. Thus, he makes pleasure a standard of value, and by inference favors optimism in preference to pessimism. We tend, he implies, to move in relative adaptation toward an ideal. An absolute ethic might be an ideal state of social harmony, he indicates, in echoing Aristotle, so that individually there would be no antagonism between altruism and selfish egoism. Spencer was enough of a scientist to realize that ideals are only approached asymptotically.

A further effort to approach moral judgments from a scientific standpoint was made by Auguste Comte (1798-1857). A mathematician, who had a precarious existence, he was supported by J.S. Mill, in his ambitious scheme of organizing knowledge into a consistent unity. The fullest life, according to Comte, is that which rests on the fullest knowledge. Spurning past theories of conduct as theological or metaphysical, he tried to interpret behavior as it is. His hierarchy of knowledge proceeded from mathematics to astronomy to physics, to chemistry, to the earth sciences, to biology, and thus to sociology. Sociology, he claimed, developed from militarism to industrialism. His moral thrust was to strengthen the social coordination of people at the expense of individual personality. Although his 6 volume *Philosophie Positive* was published from 1830 to 1842, it has a vague evolutionary flavor.

The notion of social health or social harmony was supported by Leslie Stephen (1832-1904), of Cambridge. A gentle critic and mountaineer, he left Cambridge after studying Comte, and became head of the London Ethical Society. Combining utilitarianism with an evolutionary ethic, he popularized agnosticism, and showed how utilitarian morality contributes to social evolution and social health, albeit at the expense of some individual freedom. Individual welfare, however, he claimed is to be found in social welfare. Editing the first 26 volumes of the *Dictionary of National Biography,* he also made careful studies of many English writers and poets. He failed, however, in his effort to develop ethical theory by means of a scientific methodology.

A great teacher was Thomas Hill Green (1836-1882) of Baliol College, Oxford, whose *Prolegomena to Ethics* (London, 1883) is directed along the lines of Platonic or social idealism. Emphasizing social welfare and stability as the greatest good for people, he taught that an individual's personality develops from the social conditions surrounding that person. Thus there began a breaking away from the trend of evolutionary factors in moral development, and the scene was set for its perversion.

The Power Ethic: Ruthless Superiority

To the basic question,*"What am I living for?,"* the evolutionary ethic answered, to survive by adapting to the conditions of the environment. On the surface these conditions might often appear to be rough. Darwin himself acknowledged the revelation which came to him from reading the *Essay on the Principle of Population,* issued anonymously in 1798 by Thomas Robert Malthus (1766-1834). In this it was shown that optimistic hopes for the future of humanity are made invalid by the natural tendency of human (or other animal) populations to increase more rapidly than their means of subsistence. Darwin realized "on reading Malthus *On Population* that natural selection was the inevitable result of the rapid increase of all organic beings," since such increase goes into a "struggle for existence," in which adaptation, muscular strength, or cunning may be deciding factors.

It was this aspect of evolutionary theory which seems to have fascinated that brilliant and clever fanatic, Friedrich Wilhelm Nietzsche (1844-1900). Deeply emotional, Nietzsche was yet an exceptionally keen thinker and florid writer. His classical knowledge was profound, and he served as professor of classical philology at Basel from 1869 to 1879. He was a passionate rebel, revolting against the growing intellectual socialism, and preaching an intense individualism. He was a follower of the lonely paranoid Arthur Schopenhauer (1788-1860), whose introspection led him to glorify the feelings over reason, and to insist on the supremacy of the impulses we know from inside ourselves.

Schopenhauer's notion of "will to power" inspired Nietzsche. A friend and admirer of Richard Wagner (1813-1883), whose operas he thought to be as great as the Greek tragedies, Nietzsche's first work was *Die Geburt der Tragödie* (1872) dedicated to Wagner. In this, and in his essays, *Untimely Contemplations* (1873-76) he showed his enthusiasm for the aristocratic ideal and his contempt for the common mass of people. He turned Schopenhauer's pessimism into an optimistic glorification of power. Strength favors survival, said Nietzsche, and implied that might makes right. He seems to have relished "Nature red in tooth and claw." This perversion of Darwinian principles had profound effects on the German peoples, promoting arrogance and aggressiveness, and bringing two horrible world wars. Nietzsche's own inner turmoil resulted in a mental breakdown, and he spent the last decade of his life in an asylum.

Breaking with Wagner, whose *Parsifal* disgusted him, Nietzsche violently attacked Christianity, and indeed all theo-cratic religion, proclaiming "God is dead," and extolling the virtues of a super-race. Sympathy for people in distress or misery, he claimed, merely perpetuates the mediocre and unfit. His aphoristic *Thus Spake Zarathustra* (Englished by R. J. Hollingdale, Penguin Books, Baltimore, 1961, 434 pp.) promoted the concept of the egoistical superman, rejoicing in his power and ruthlessness. In *Beyond Good and Evil* (1886) Nietzsche expounded the notion that nothing is true, and everything is permissible (to one's conscience). Suffering, he claimed, is insignificant, especially among slaves, since what we call "higher culture is based on the spiritualizing and intensifying of cruelty." Here seems to be the beginning of Buchenwald and other Nazi atrocities, of the sadistic excesses of the Italian Fascists, and of other authoritarian regimes as Russia under Stalin. It also may be, along with Machiavellian ruthlessness, the background for USA heartlessness, as at Mai Lai.

In the *Genealogy of Morals* of 1887 (Englished by Francis Golfing, along with *The Birth of Tragedy*, Doubleday, Garden City, New York, 1956, 299 pp.), Nietzsche offers much perceptive etymological and psychological insight. He wrote superbly: even in English, his thoughts blaze. He is very persuasive. Yet, there is a strange impression that he protests too much. The third essay asking what ascetic ideals mean, goes on, cleverly, and with much sharp insight, to conclude that we would sooner have the void for a purpose than be void of purpose. Here is the substance of the long existentialist revolt against social rationality.

The Existential Ethic: Emotional Impulse

In his *Irrational Man* (Doubleday, Garden City, New York, 1962, 314 pp.), William Barrett of New York University offers a perceptive lucid study of current existential philosophy. The assault of the emotions on our intelligence began early. Primitive religions throve on it; the ancient Greeks enjoyed it (See E. R. Dodds, *The Greeks and the Irrational,* Beacon Press, Boston, 1957, 327 pp.); it was the basis for the Christian Church, and even after the Reformation, there remained a general popular belief in witchcraft and demonology. That there is so much current irrationality now, as revealed in popular interest in astrology, extra-sensory perception, black magic, yoga, encounter groups, "mind-expansion" (usually with drugs), and esoteric symbolism, should not be surprising: it has always occurred when mass intelligence, the intellectual effort of ordinary people, cannot keep up with the scientific demonstrations or technical applications with which we are flooded.

The three great scientific movements of recent centuries, Galileo's mechanics, culminating in Newton's gravitational cosmology, Darwin's adaptational evolutionary theory, and Einstein's relativity, were generally beyond the comprehension of common people. They then took refuge in what they thought they could understand, witchcraft in the 17th Century, romanticism and impressionism in the 19th Century, and a mess of mysticism in our own. The interesting paradox is that there developed a powerful intellectual effort to justify this popular anti-intellectualism. This occurred through the growth of existentialism, with Soren Gaby Kierkegaard (1813-1855), the guilt-ridden, love-renouncing Copenhagen theologian; Nietzsche; Martin Heidegger (1899-   ), the obscure Nazi thinker; and Jean-Paul Sartre (1905-   ), the left-wing Parisian dramatist and novelist.

As Professor Barrett shows, and as Nietzsche indicated, the existential problem had its origin in the clash between Hebraic emotionalism and Hellenic intellectualism, or in the conflict between the primitive, sensory, matriarchal, orgiastic cult of

Dionysius, and the patriarchal, sun-lit emotionally controlled, and intellectual cult of Apollo. In his clear discussion of Hebraism and Hellenism, Barrett contrasts the Hebraic faith in God with Aristotle's claim that one's rational self is one's real self, pointing out that the Church in medieval Europe, placed faith at the supernatural center of one's personality, with reason at one's natural center.

Later, in returning to the Dionysisian-Apollonian clash among the Greeks, Barrett notes neatly the significance of the great Oresteia trilogy of Aeschylus (525-456 B. C.). In the final drama, the *Eumenides,* the choice had to be made between the old matriarchal deities of gut reactions, such as Dionysius, and the new Olympic patriarchal deities of reasoned responsibility, such as Apollo; a choice between the subconscious psychological drives within us, and conscious reason. The vote was a tie; thanks to Athena, the ambiguous goddess of wisdom, Orestes is freed from the vengeance of the Furies (for murdering his mother at Apollo's urging) and the Furies are placated by having a sanctuary reserved for them and by giving them the protection of children. Barrett wisely notes that the Furies cannot be bought off, even by tranquilizers or sleeping pills, but are appeased by the respect due them, dark, powerful and primitive as they are. Even at the core of the light of a rational enlightenment there is also a dark spot.

Kierkegaard saw this. In his renunciation of his Regina and a conventional life, he realized the choice he was making for his whole future. This had to be lived through and directly experienced. The crux of any ethical dilemma is an existence-making choice, his famed *Either/Or* (1843) decision. Many people have more of a fear of making a decision than of the consequences thereof. It may well be that "decidophobia" is a psychiatric disorder brought about by the same kinds of conditioning that may result in other phobias.

Although Nietzsche brilliantly advocated a gut-reaction power ethic, he did so intellectually. The Nazis applied this ethic directly, without bothering about intellectualizing it. They did, however rationalize it, in the sense of excusing it. It was a hypocritical means to despicable ends. Heidegger was concerned with moral choices, but his language is so obscure that one comes up with nothing. That is apparently what he thought living was about. Sartre seems to say that one is no more than one's committments, and that despair and anguish go with choice, as the price of freedom. This was Kierkegaard's "fear and trembling and dread." Sartre echoes Nietzsche in proclaiming God to be dead, and thus in saying we have to rely on ourselves with our faulty wills and insights.

As Barrett points out, existentialism pervades our art, music, literature, poetry and drama. All our humanistic effort seems to be directed against intellectual control, against the cold verifiability of scientific consensus, against the actual and potential ruinous applications of our scientific knowledge in our ever-growing monstrous technology, and against the applications of scientific knowledge to our ever-more crushing bureaucratic regulation of life.

As an extreme example of this existential revolt one might consider the opera by Kurt Weil (1900-1950) and Bertolt Brecht (1898-1956), *The Rise and Fall of the City of Mahogonny* (1930). In this, a group of escaped criminals establishes a remote USA community where anything is permitted as long as it is paid for. Many flock to it, even though death is the penalty for not being able to pay for what one wants to do. Ironically, the staging includes the most sophisticated technological devices, most of which detract from the episodic play.

It may be observed that the tension of existentialism, the ambivalence in each of us, between our emotions and our intellect, is a variant on the medieval legend of Faust. This was given its most detailed and philosophical treatment by Johann Wolfgang von Goethe (1749-1832), in his great drama, Faust, (1808-1832). Goethe himself, though tormented quite as much as Kierkegaard and Nietzsche, in his emotional life, found refuge in scientific endeavor, and became the symbol of German liberalism as opposed to the Prussian arrogant nationalism and militarism.

As we shall see, existentialism, with its emphasis on emotional subjective feeling, and its negation of rational intellectual effort, and its rejection of verifiable knowledge and its applications, as in science and technology, has undermined the traditional standards of our arts and humanities. Then Charles P. Snow can bewail the two cultures, and motivation to harmonize them is lost.

The Professional Ethic: Pragmatism

Meanwhile, new voices from the New World began to be heard in the ethical debate. They were clear and plausible. William James (1842-1910), a physician, began at Harvard, to put psychology on a physiological basis. His classic *Principles of Psychology* (Henry Holt, New York, 1890, 2 Vols.) firmly established the subject as a scientific discipline. James was himself a hard-headed scientist on the one hand and a soft-hearted gentleman on the other. His psychological study on *The Will to Believe* (Longmans Green, New York, 1897) popularized the idea of wishful-thinking, and indicated the power of conditioned motivation. His "study in human nature," *The Varieties of Religious Experience* (Longmans Green, New York, 1902; Collier Books, New York, 1961, 416 pp.) was given as the Gifford Lectures in Edinburgh. His first lecture, "Religion and Neurology," showed the psycho-pathetic aspects of many religious experiences. He was clearly sympathetic to what he called "religions of healthy-mindedness." His general philosophy was outlined in his *Pragmatism: A New Name for Some Old Ways of Thinking* (Longmans Green, New York, 1907; Meridian Books, Cleveland, Ohio, 1955, 269 pp.; Washington Square Press, New York, 1963, 313 pp.,).

In an address to the Yale Philosophical Club *(Internat. J. Ethics,* April, 1891), James talked on "The Moral Life." He began by stating, "There is no such thing as an ethical philosophy made up in advance. We all help to determine the content of ethical philosophy so far as we contribute to the race's moral life ...There can be no final truth in ethics any more than in physics." This clear flat declaration is characteristic of James. It is not really as dogmatic as it may sound. It was based on his experience and his reflection thereon, an intellectual process inculcated in his medical training. This was his "pragmatic" intellectual procedure: From reflection on his emotional and intellectual experiences, and on his careful observation of the behavior of others, he could induce the general principle that a proposition that works toward the purpose desired is better than one that does not. This often requires trial or experiment, at least in imagination, in figuring the consequences of a proposed act in comparison with the consequences of other actions. It is thus utilitarian in one sense, and empirical in another. James dedicated his *Pragmatism* "To the memory of John Stuart Mill from whom I first learned the pragmatic openness of mind."

James' development of pragmatism was influenced in part by his mathematical colleague, Charles Sanders Peirce (1839-1914), who was much of a recluse. James took from Peirce the notion that what is true or good is that which is agreed upon to be so by those who investigate it, either in general or in specific instances. James was also greatly stimulated by discussions with his colleague, Josiah Royce (1855-1916), the California idealist, who emphasized individual dignity, and stressed its value in any social grouping. James opposed any metaphysical system, and called himself a radical empiricist. His general position was that beliefs do not work because they are true, but rather that they are true (or good) because they do work. This is the professional ethic.

Consider the recent ethical furor over organ transplants, usually kidney, sometimes bone marrow. The intended recipient is motivated hedonistically, thinking of the joy of continuing to live; the donor, usually a relative or friend, was (cadaver use puts the problem in the past!) motivated by an altruistic social idealism, in doing something for someone else, even at personal sacrifice, while the operating team of surgeons, nurses, and internists are chiefly concerned, pragmatically, with the success of the operation, with having it work. Here, then, in the same situation, was a clash between three different, usually unrecognized, ethical theories.

Any of these moral formulations might fail effectively to carry through: the hedonist might get qualms of conscience, and develop a guilt complex, especially if death approaches; the idealist may regret giving up some valuable organ, and immunological rejection may cause the operation to fail, even though technically successful. As I have suggested, under these possible consequences, it would seem wise for patient, donor, surgeon, psychiatrist, intern, family and lawyer to get together, and agree in advance on that to which they would in good faith remain committed.

Fortunately, organ banks have now been developed for ear-ossicles, corneas and lenses of eyes, kidneys, marrow, and even sperm (a new kind of life insurance), as well as the long established blood banks. We may even be getting artificial organs, such as kidneys (so that the moral problem of when to stop expensive dialysis machines because of lack of funds will no longer bother us), and even nuclear powered artificial hearts. As we age we may become more and more a conglomerate of spare parts! In the dark background to all of this is the prevailing fear of death, repressed to the subconscious, where it often breeds distress. We would be wise to realize that life may not be worth living when our individual genetic span has run its course. Then we console ourselves with the reflection that we really become part of our precarious species.

As the usual, if unconscious, professional ethic, pragmatism operates among lawyers, engineers, scientists, members of the various health professions, churchmen, and the military. Their basic interest is in getting their professional function to work; if it does, it is good. Thus this gets close in practice to Nietzsche's power ethic. James, I think, would deplore this, realizing that pragmatism can be fully justified only if it is fully responsible to individuals and to society. The professions are necessary functional groups in social organization, but to serve society satisfactorily, they must remain subject to social control.

Pragmatism is an ethic of practicality. It appeals to activists, but is suspected by existentialists as being oriented toward technology. Anti-intellectuals of all varieties dislike the pragmatic ethic because it encourages objective and rational evaluations, whereas they would prefer subjective validity alone. It is to James' credit that he recognized the force of both points of view, but realized also that it is one's total experience up to any one moment in life that tends to position one's view, either outward toward others, or inward toward oneself. Pragmatism works either way: what works for any one individual tends to be thought of as "good" by that individual. What works for social welfare, if that is the purpose of a group, depends on the consensus of the group.

The Ethic of Responsibility

It is noteworthy that analysis of the ethic of responsibility, first emphasized in relation to the Big Boss, as exemplified in the Book of Job, should arise again in our times. It is a sort of echoed remembrance of a racial childhood experience. Yet, for our time, it is especially pertinent since there is such a proliferation of Big Bosses, in business, in politics, in government, in huge trade unions, in large corporations, in schools, in professions, in churches. In all there is the recurring scandal of the Big Boss profiting individually at the collective expense of the group which made that person its Big Boss.

There is then much general concern over the problem of how to keep the Big Boss responsible in fulfilling the obligations of the position. It is the general assumption that the primary obligation of the Big Boss of any group is the promotion of the welfare of that group, even at self-sacrifice of the Big Boss's individual welfare. It does not go well with the ordinary members of the group when the Big Boss lives in a conspicuous luxury denied to them. Dictators, union leaders,and all Big Bosses would be wise to consider the ethics of social idealism, hedonism, utilitarianism, pragmatism, and obligation.

Influential in the 19th Century discussion of an obligation ethic was Thomas Hill Green (1836-1882), White's professor of moral philosophy at Oxford. To him, the social group to which an individual belongs is what is paramount in shaping that individual's personality. Since that social group trusts that individual to strive for that group's welfare, that individual has the obligation of justifying that trust. Psychologically there is much hedonistic pleasure, or satisfaction, in justifying that trust. The concept of "duty" in this sense becomes a powerful moral force, as Green showed in his *Prolegomenon to Ethics*. (1883)

The obligation ethic was analyzed in greater detail by George Edward Moore (1873-1958), the distinguished Cambridge champion of "common sense," who greatly influenced Bertrand Russell (1872-1970). Moore was a skilled logician and a pioneer semanticist, concerned with the meaning of such common terms as "good" or "goodness." He took the position that the word "good" or "goodness" is not satisfactorily defined in terms of natural qualities, such as pleasure, pain, aggressiveness, submissiveness, useful, harmful, or similar antithetic concepts. He showed that whichever of these qualities are taken to define "good," it makes sense to ask whether anyone or anything possessing them is "good." This is a subtle but important point, and focuses on the basic moral problems of what is good for what. The basic question for each of us, *"What am I living for?,"* at once involves purposes, motivations, general or specific goals, and interpersonal relations. Moore's analysis appears in his *Principia Ethica* (Cambridge University Press, 1903, frequently reprinted; in paperback six times since 1959, 232 pp.).

Moore was interested in what things and what actions are usually agreed upon as being "good," and for what purpose. Also of interest to him were what purposes are generally agreed upon as being "good." The obligation to justify a trust may be agreed upon as "good," but trusting someone to act in any way harmful to others, or even to oneself, may not be "good." And what do we mean by "harmful?" Here the way was being prepared, although probably sub-or un-consciously, for important later developments in ethical theory.

British ethical writers during the latter part of the 19th

Century and first part of the 20th Century were solidly rational. Francis Herbert Bradley (1846-1924) of Oxford, was sharply critical of ethical postulates and assumptions, and he influenced Bertrand Russell. Alfred Edward Taylor (1869-1945), professor of moral philosophy at St. Andrews and Edinburgh, refused to permit metaphysical speculation to be part of ethical formulation. In *The Problem of Conduct* (1901), he finds a constant dualism in morality, which reduces to the opposition between egoism and altruism. The ethics, he claims, deserve to be part of a positive or experimental study, rather than merely speculative. He finds a basis for ethics in the facts of human life as revealed by psychological and sociological investigation. Leonard Trelaway Hobhouse (1864-1929) of Oxford, and later sociologist at the University of London, wrote on evolutionary factors in morality, as in his *Morals in Evolution* (1906) and *Development and Purpose* (1913). He viewed moral formulations as an outgrowth of the conditioning of functional activity, and of the choice of purposes.

A British ethicist who subjected moral obligation to the sharpest scrutiny, was Harold Arthur Prichard (1871-1947), one of the Oxford group who put high value on one's "intuition." This seems to be the ability some people have, especially women, to reach valid conclusions so rapidly that the thought chains are not conscious. Prichard's essays and lectures have been collected in a small volume entitled *Moral Obligation* (Oxford University Press, 1968, 239 pp.,). This contains his inaugural lecture as White's professor of moral philosophy on "Duty and Interest." In this he claims that the notion of "duty" depends not on the actual situation, but on what one believes it to be. There are, he notes, different degrees of compulsiveness in obligations. Rightness, he says, is not dependent on motive, but rather on interest, as far as an individual goes. The social judgment on the "good" of an act is again dependent on what the group believes the circumstances to be. One cannot derive an "ought" from one's concept of a "good," he concludes, but both remain intuitive.

The younger American moralists reflect Moore's logical semanticism. Thus Kurt Erick Brier (1917-   ), of Vienna, Melbourne, and Pittsburgh, tackles the problem of responsibility from the standpoint of freewill. Scientific evidence seems to indicate, according to a deterministic position, that everything, including one's "will" is causally determined. Under this idea, no one is to be blamed for anything, and thus punishment is never deserved, however legitimate. The concept of responsibility, however, is derived from the long social practice of holding people to account for what they do. It is thus a safeguard, in a way, of maintaining individual compliance with social custom, and of protecting individuals from the capriciousness of others.

Brier finds four ways in which moral responsibility may be considered: as accountable, as answerable, as culpable, and as liable. He also considers the morality of coercion, either by external force, a compulsion by circumstances, or compulsion from within. Responsibility would seem to be involved chiefly in the latter. For a neat summary of Brier's position, see his essay, "Responsibility and Freedom" in *Ethics and Society,* well arranged by Richard T. DeGeorge (1933-   ), of the University of Kansas (Doubleday Anchor Books, Garden City, New York, 1966, pp. 49-84).

Errol E. Harris, also of the University of Kansas, in developing the moral notion of obligation, or of justifying a trust, has reference to the respect due to all persons including ourselves, by virtue of our common humanity. In this view all of us are ends in our individual selves, and none are justifiable means to anyone else's ends. He considers an obligation to act to be a form of self-imposed constraint regardless of inclination. He uses St. Paul's exhortation to Philemon as an illustration of basic respect for a person: Paul sends Onesimus back to his master, "no longer a slave, but as a dear brother." Again, for a neat summary of Harris's position, see his essay, "Respect for Persons," in Richard DeGeorge's anthology, *Ethics and Society* (Doubleday Anchor Books, Garden City, New York, 1966, pp. 111-132).

The Ecological Ethic

This notion of the respect due (the "duty" of respect) to all persons, including oneself, can be and has been extended to all living things, to everything partaking of that exquisitely delicate balance called "life." Pioneering in this extension of respect to all living things was that reformed rake, heretical mystic and later saint, Francis of Assisi (1181-1226). As my Bohemian Club friend, Lynn White, showed in a perceptive essay, "Historical Roots of Our Ecological Crisis," *(Science,* March 10, 1967), St. Francis was a deeply religious, but probably an unconscious and certainly unrecognized heretic, flaunting conspicuously one of the first general commandments given in the Hebraic myth of creation. As given in Genesis 1:26 and 28, God, having created the world and all living things, made a man, and gave him "dominion over all living things." This injunction was repeated, even before the making of a woman; "Be fruitful and multiply, and replenish the earth and subdue it, and have dominion over every living thing that moveth on the earth."

This command, being taken literally, has been followed in Judeo-Christian cultures ever since, and seems to have become an ingrained dogma among people with a Judeo-Christian background. It has justified the despoiling of lands and waters ever since, with the wanton destruction of any kind of life which people did not want, or might be in their way. It has led to the extinction of many living species, both plant and animal, none of which can ever again, in accordance with the thermodynamic principle of entropy, reappear in our environment. The full significance of this deliberate, even though gradual and fragmentary, destruction of the ecological balances from which we evolved, is only now beginning to be realized. St. Francis seems to have sensed it, and to have preached vigorously against it. His tender example seems equally to have been unavailing.

The concept, "reverence for all life," became fully formulated by the famed Alsatian organist, musicologist, and theologian, Albert Schweitzer (1875-1967). In his *Geschichte der Leben-Jesu Forschung* (1913, translated as *The Quest for the Historical Jesus*), he had analyzed the ethical teachings of Jesus, making their motivation dependent on belief in the possibility of "heaven on earth." Having studied medicine, and being qualified as a physician, he married a devoted scholar, and went with her to organize a hospital in an abandoned mission in Lambarene, on the Ogowe River in then French Equatorial Africa. Here he ministered effectively and paternalistically to the natives, getting them to build hospital and laboratory facilities, and to help in caring for his many patients.

Many fund raising trips to Europe kept Schweitzer in touch with current thought. A sympathetic appreciation of him and of his amazing activity may be found in Herman Hagedorn's *Albert Schweitzer: Prophet in the Wilderness,* (Collier Books, New York 1962, 234 pp.) A comprehensive biography of Schweitzer has been prepared by George Marshall and David Poling (Doubleday, New York, 1972, 320 pp.) At the Aspen Institute evaluation conference on Schweitzer's influence, after his death, I was glad that I could pay tribute to Helene Bresslau, his ever-helpful wife, who so carefully edited his writings, and to Erica Kellner Anderson, who so brilliantly filmed his hospital work.

Schweitzer's ethical principle of reverence for all life was developed in reference to the manifold defects of European civilization in two books: *Verfall und Wiederaufbau der Kultur* and *Kultur and Ethik,* both published in 1923, and promptly translated. Though widely honored (he was Hibbert Lecturer at Oxford and London in 1934, and Gifford Lecturer at Edinburgh in 1935, and awarded the Nobel Peace Prize in 1952), and although he was voluminously written about, it cannot be claimed that his ethical ideas made much of a popular impact. They were certainly well discussed, but the ancient legendary command to take dominion over all life was too firmly implanted in western peoples to permit popular interest.

This attitude of subduing the earth and all life on it was dramatically changed by the appearance of *Silent Spring*

(Houghton, Mifflin & Co., Boston, 1962, 320 pp.), by the modest, quiet, and brilliant biologist and writer, Rachel Louise Carson (1907-1964). Her book popularly dramatized the delicacy of the ecological balance and how easily and dangerously we disturb it. She showed the devastating effects of the over-extensive use of agricultural insecticides in the chain reaction from insects to birds, and on.

The editor of Rachel Carson's classics, *Silent Spring* and *The Sea Around Us,* has given a detailed account of the storm of abuse which broke over her at the appearance of *Silent Spring.* Paul Brooks, in *The House of Life* (Houghton, Mifflin and Co., Boston, 1972, 310 pp.) gave a justified indictment of the ruthless greed of many great commercial companies. The attempt to discredit Rachel Carson was instigated by the huge chemical concerns which were making immense profits from the wide sale of insecticides for pest control in the growing industrialization of agriculture. From these same big companies come the phosphate and nitrogen fertilizers, the over-use of which brings run-off into waterways, which promote clogging algal growth. This uses up the oxygen, and fish and all life dies, as in Lake Erie. Another horrible example of ruthless destruction of natural beauty is the devastation of majestic California redwood groves by absentee lumber barons. Against this despoiling of our natural heritage, the Sierra Club and other conservation groups are slowly making progress.

Many other competent investigators, in addition to Rachel Carson, drove home the proposition that we can destroy all life too easily by the technological power we now have, as emphasized by Barry Commoner. Disastrous pollution of airs and water endangers all life, ours included, and environmental preservation and conservation are becoming strong popular movements. Fortunately our youngsters are interested, but too often their zeal goes off in fads, such as "organic foods."

The awful power of nuclear energy, as revealed in the bombing of Hiroshima and Nagasaki in 1945, made all people everywhere, aware of the potential danger of destroying us all. The unfortunate "cold war" and "arms race" intensified this universal fear. This resulted in further widespread discontent,

especially among young people, at the immoral and potentially destructive effects of technology. The rebellion focussed
against scientific effort, and anti-intellectualism flourishes.

Theodore Roszak has well described *The Making of a
Counter-Culture* (Doubleday Anchor Books, Garden City,
New York, 1969, 313 pp.). The profound disillusionment with
the professed idealism of the USA, which so terribly floundered in Vietnam, and which began after World War II with
the vicious reactionary tyranny of McCarthyism together with
racist abuse, had thoroughly alienated our young people. In
throngs they flocked to expressions of existentialism and
found nothing there also. Rock music and the shambles of
outdoor pop festivals flamed the huge discontent, and the
revolt on our campuses, the presumed citadels of intellect and
reason, reached violent heights. Fortunately for all, the
dawning ecological ethic has attracted the attention of our
young intellectuals. They have found something worthy to fuss
over, whether in miniparks, Cretan caves, or the heights of
Nepal, rather than with drugs, astrology, Zen and other fads.

Fortunately for us, international efforts are being made by
our responsible government officials, to obtain intergovern-
mental cooperation among nations directed toward peace and
general human welfare. Under President Richard Nixon of the
USA, promising understandings are being reached with China
and Russia over future cooperation directed toward peaceful
benefit to all people. One would have thought that whole-
hearted support of the United Nations by all governments
would be a clear way to achieve the commonly professed goal
of peace and welfare for all people. It is interesting that it is in
the free exchange of scientific information that most progress
seems to be made, both under bilateral agreements and the
United Nations. Science does imply freedom and general
social and individual welfare, as I tried to show long ago.

The Individualistic Ethic

Rejecting social customs or even obligations, the existential movement of the past century plunged toward individualism, introspection, and anti-intellectualism. It was sharply curbed, for a while, by the consideration of individual responsibility, first to oneself, and then by reflection to others. This was the old discovery of the Greek hedonists. Now it took a more sophisticated slant. Hedonism, in one form or another, seems ever to have fascinated English moralists, however they might disguise it as utilitarianism. They have become wearisome in their hair-splitting logical and semantic analyses of the words used in ethical discussion.

One can readily note this in the essays collected by Philippa Foote, under the misleading title, *Theories of Ethics,* (Oxford University Press, 1967, 188 pp.) In this series of twelve essays three are commentaries on John Stuart Mill and utilitarianism. W. D. Hudson's *Modern Moral Philosophy* (Doubleday Anchor Books, Garden City, New York, 1970, 370 pp.) is a detailed semantic discussion of what people are doing when they *talk* about what they ought to do.

The problem raised by David Hume, about the difference between "ought" and "is" still bothers us. R. M. Hare of Oxford devotes a full book, *The Language of Morals* (Oxford University Press, 1964, 202 pp.) to the semantic details of the words commonly used by moral philosophers. All of this semantic effort might be helpful if agreement could be reached on what ethical terminology would mean to all who use it. This does not seem to be the case. Thus disagreement over principles, and popular confusion, continue. Individual judgment on individual values is the vogue, and social obligations tend to languish.

A common-sense approach to an individualistic ethic was offered by Warner Fite (1867-1955), who was my teacher in ethics at Princeton. His writings abound in the practical illustrations of moral problems in everyday life. His *Individualism* (Columbia University Press, 1911, 212 pp.) emphasized the importance of self-consciousness with self-criticism in interpersonal relationships. He amplified this viewpoint in

The Examined Life (Indiana University Press, 1957, 276 pp.) taking as his text Socrates' remark in the *Apology* that the unexamined life is not fit for living. Fite insists that morality is self-conscious living, that is in knowing what one is doing. He thus raises the basic question for us all, *"What am I living for?"*

Fite differentiates morality from ethics, by pointing out that, whereas morality is a way of life, ethics are studies of morality, studies of meanings and values of living. To him morality is a product of intelligence, of an examined life. Morality is not so much a matter of what is arbitrarily right or wrong, as it is the result of a critical examination of one's way of life. Studies of morality, he says, yield two classes of ethical theory (1) an absolutist or authoritarian type, in which morality is based on an authority assumed to be superior to one's individual choice, as is in the case of the Big Boss theory, or in the ethical derivations from Newton, and (2) a humanistic type, in which morality is derived from human nature, and human choice, as in hedonism, utilitarianism, or pragmatism. To these two basic types, others may be added, as I have tried to indicate.

Robert G. Olson, at Rutgers University in Jew Jersey, has well analyzed *The Morality of Self-Interest* (Harcourt, Brace and World, New York, 1965, 188 pp.) in a manner relating an individualistic ethic to the welfare of society. He shows that one's self-interest is part of the interest of the group to which one belongs. Personal ethics, he says, cannot be divided from questions of social policy. He goes on to state that an act cannot be considered to be wholly right unless it promotes the well-being of both the agent and society, and that one is most likely to contribute to social betterment by rationally pursuing one's own best long-range interests. Further, he claims that rational procedures of the sort employed in the empirical sciences are in principle competent to define moral terms and determine the truth or falsehood of moral judgments. Prevailing religious views, he believes, are not conducive to moral uprightness. He considers the conflict between duty and desire. His clear rationality is referred to individual and social well-being and to the promotion of moral responsibility.

Individualistic ethics have been extended by Abraham Maslow (1908-1971), of Brandeis University and the Laughlin Foundation of Menlo Park, California. His plea is for individuals to fulfill themselves, to make the most of their abilities and circumstances in what he calls "self-actualization." His is a call to the full life; for enjoyment of living by utilizing one's talents to the fullest for long-range fitting into one's community. As a skilled psychologist, he explores motivations in the development of personality, especially from the standpoint of fulfilling one's capabilities. As with Fite and Olsen, Maslow's individualism is coordinated with an interdependent socialism. The welfare of an individual seems always to be in varying ways dependent on the welfare of the group to which that individual belongs, and vice-versa.

Maslow makes much of "peak experiences," in which strong emotional reactions of ecstasy or grief can bring moving insights of moral significance. In this he resembles Teilhard de Chardin (1881-1955), the Jesuit anthropologist, who emphasizes the ethical significance of "illumination." They both make much of the feeling of awe, humility, wonder and mystery which comes over us when we confront, without understanding, some impressive phenomenon. Even the most objectively oriented and detached scientists may experience this feeling. The similarities in Maslow's and Chardin's points of view have been well explored by Weston A. Stevens (*Religious Humanism,* 6: 15-19, 1972). In such an experience, they say, persons may get a better sense of their own identity, a more accurate feeling of what it is like really to feel oneself. Thus one may be able to transcend one's petty needs and be less selfish, and more loving, and accepting. A "peak experience" is gratifying, and one then needs less, is more relaxed, and strives for less. This sounds a bit like Saul's "conversion" on the road to Damascus, or like most people feel after a sexual orgasm. It also sounds like the excesses made popular by Aldous Huxley (1894-1968) for using hallucinating drugs. (*The Doors of Perception and Heaven and Hell,* Harper, 1963, 185 pp.)

Individual morality is not, as Fite showed, the same as an individualistic ethic. Yet the latter may justify the former. To avoid chaos and anarchy, however, only such individual morality is really justified which takes into consideration the welfare of those with whom one is in relationship, as well as oneself.

The New Sex Ethic

As yet, the majority of the USA citizens, certainly the Wasps (White Anglo-Saxon Protestants), consider sex synonymous with sin, and thus the mores of sexual activity are a predominant part of conventional morality. In this same majority, ethics has a wider connotation, so that it includes "conflict of interest." One would suppose that only a little reflection would bring these people to realize that sexual activity is merely one aspect of life in which general ethical principles are applicable. But no, most of our citizenry still thinks that morality is chiefly concerned with sexual activity, and the words commonly used in connection therewith.

This is a remarkable hangover from times long past. It is a reflection of the Zoroastrian identification of women with darkness and evil; of the ascetic Essenic total rejection of women; of the Pauline strictures against women, and the dogma that any sexual activity except that associated with procreation is evil; of the puritannical strictures of the Calvinists, and of the grossly hypocritical Victorian sexual morality. There had, of course, been many reactions: the bawdiness of the Greek comedies; the licentiousness of the Romans; the monastic scandals; the chivalrous medieval glorification of women; the Restoration excesses in England, and the underground pornography of the Victorian era. Through all these ups and downs of sex mores in Europe, the old Chinese and Hindu cultures went their calm ways, sexual activity being considered to be merely an ordinary aspect of ordinary living, gradually to be relegated to anecdotage. It is interesting that although the Russians are as lusty and as earthy as any people anywhere, they nevertheless are remarkably uptight officially on sexual matters. Peasants generally are this way also, whenever they are in the presence of strangers.

The Victorian hangup on sex was marked in the USA, with extensive legal penalties for any sort of extra-marital sex activity, and even for "perversion" in the marriage relationship. The relatively more realistic and pragmatic approach to sexual affairs, characteristic of European peoples, was pleasantly "shocking" to tourists from the USA, who indulged themselves greedily, to the profit (and disdain) of their hosts. It was this hypocritical attitude which led the Cubans to despise the Americans, and which now threatens the good-will of the Puerto Ricans.

Exploitation of gambling inevitably goes along with exploitation of sex. Similarly, exploitation of alcoholic beverages and addictive drugs is part of the picture. It is significant in the USA that this combination of activities is called "vice." Confusion over morals and ethics is thus assured, especially when gross venality and corruption of public officials makes the prohibitive laws on "vice" un-enforceable, and the laws themselves a mockery.

It is significant that a strong movement is under way in the USA to repeal "victimless laws." Upon our consciousness is dawning the fact that society is now so vast and complex that uniform laws governing "victimless" behavior are no longer workable. Small in-groups can more effectively set and enforce their codes of conduct, if they so wish. Our legal system is such that individuals considering themselves to have been "victimized," may sue the presumed offenders, as in the case of breach-of-promise.

There is growing popular concern over the simple fact, from long experience, that moral laws don't work. Charles McCabe, the "fearless spectator" of the *San Francisco Chronicle* reported on April 3, 1972, the opinion of the large membership of the California Probation Parole and Correctional Association in support of a statement by the National Council on Crime and Delinquency:

> Laws creating "crimes without victims" should be removed from criminal codes. They are based not on harm done to others but on legislatively declared moral standards that condemn behavior in which there is no victim or in which the only one hurt is the person behaving.

The commonest examples of such so-called crimes are

drunkenness, drug addiction, homosexual and other voluntary sex acts, vagrancy, gambling and prostitution, and among children, truancy and running away from home.

The report goes on to show the ineffectiveness of such laws, and the disrespect in which they are held. It demonstrates how legal penalties produce no changes in the behavior of the persons penalized. Further the prosecution of such cases clogs the courts, and promotes widespread police and racketeering corruption as "protection" from prosecution. For these persons, the appropriate measures are not the futile and destructive sanctions imposed by police, or court, or jail, but rather the voluntary services offered by a medical or social agency.

How did the stern puritanical Victorian sex mores change so dramatically and quickly? This was chiefly the result of the skilled writing of four keen thinkers: Sigmund Freud (1859-1939), the brilliant Vienna neurologist; Henry Havelock Ellis (1856-1939), the well traveled English physician; Bertrand Russell (1872-1970), the greatest logician of our time, and David Herbert Lawrence (1885-1930), the tuberculous traveler and novelist. Three were English, and Freud spent his last years in London, a refugee from the Nazis. Of these, Freud was the most influential, Russell the most rational, and Ellis the first in shocking the Victorian world into a realization of the actual significance of public attitudes on sexual affairs.

Havelock Ellis, who was a pioneer in studying the pharmacological effects of hallucinating agents, such as mescal or peyote, compiled seven volumes of *Studies in the Psychology of Sex,* published in London from 1897 to 1928. These were the first objective systematic psychological and sociological investigations of the subject, free from both sensationalism and emotional reflections of guilt. They caused much controversy at first, but now are almost forgotten in the flood of sensational and often prurient writings on the problem. Actually Havelock Ellis's effort was first successfully extended by the careful survey of sexual activity among a selected group of USA men and women by the modest and meticulous Indiana biologist, Alfred Charles Kinsey (1894-1956). His analyzed data were incorporated in two misnamed books, *Sexual Behavior in the Human Male* (W. B. Saunders, Philadelphia, 1948) and *Sexual Behavior in the Human Female,* issued in 1953. These are misnamed, in my opinion, because they deal with very small samples of USA men and women, and blithely neglect billions of others. Conclusions drawn from these books are referrable only to the population sampled. These indicate, however, the wide extent of sexual activity in which many people engage.

A more detailed laboratory study of physiological reactions during sexual intercourse was made by William Howell Masters (1915-   ) and Virginia Eshelman Johnson (1925-   ). They later married. Their book attracted wide attention (*Human Sexual Behavior*, Little, Brown and Co., Boston, 1966). The international interest in, and aspects of, human sexuality were explored in much detail by some 300 scientists and physicians at *Symposium Sexualogicum, Pragense* (Charles University, Prague, 1969, 305 pp.). This volume indicates the worldwide interest in sexual problems in relation to various aspects of conventional sex mores.

A major contributor to modern psychology, especially in regard to sexual morality, was that remarkably humanistic Viennese physician, Sigmund Freud (1856-1939). Trained as a physiologist and neurologist, he became fascinated by the study of hysteria, in which he succeeded in affording relief by promoting a mental catharsis. This work, with Josef Breuer (1842-1925), was published in 1895, and has had careful English translation by James Strachey, (Basic Books, New York, 1957, 335 pp.). Freud was convinced that infantile desires, mostly sexual, are suppressed by brain activity as an individual reacts to a social environment.

In 1900 Freud published on the interpretation of dreams, comparing them with neuroses in that they are disguised manifestations of repressed wishes, usually of sexual origin. He showed that there is a vast reservoir of emotional, irrational, sensuous brain activity, which he called the Id. This corresponds to what we refer to as the activity of the brain stem. Consciousness incorporates this into the personality of an individual, the Ego. The general inhibitory activity of the cortical areas of the brain, as shown by the pioneer Russian physiologist, Ivan Michaelovich Sechenov (1829-1905), comprises the Super-ego, or conscience of a person. It is here that the emotional disturbance of guilt arises. Freud developed a painstaking methodology, psycho-analysis, a greatly expanded confessional, to relieve the tension and its symptoms.

Freud's humanistic skill as a writer, and the popularization of his works, brought about a veritable revolution in the conventional sex mores of Judeo-Christian culture. This was expanded in many ways. Detailed clinical studies of sex pathology became popularly available. An early example, published in 1885, was *Psychopathia Sexualis* (English edition, Putnam's, New York, 1965, 640 pages), by Richard Kraft-Ebing (1840-1902), professor of psychiatry at Vienna. After World War I, social mores on sex affairs had so relaxed that a flood of hitherto surreptitious sex-oriented novels and other pornographic material surfaced.

While much of this had wide undercover circulation in Europe and England, the censorship in the USA was exceedingly severe. This was chiefly the result of the fanaticism of Anthony Comstock (1844-1915), an idealistic Civil War veteran, who organized the New York Society for the Suppression of Vice in 1873. He became Post-office Inspector that same year, assuming power to censor all mail, with regard to what he considered to be harmful to morals. He boasted that he had "brought to justice" a total of 3,670 persons for sending salacious material through the mail, and had destroyed 160 tons of obscene literature and pictures.

The item which finally broke this remarkable censorship was the rather earthy, but good-willed novel, *Lady Chatterly's Lover,* issued in Florence in 1924, by the tuberculous David Herbert Lawrence (1885-1930). A long series of court actions finally resulted in a marked loosening of restrictions on what was never satisfactorily defined as "obscenity." The pendulum has now swung to the extreme of license, with vulgar commercialization of "porno shops," "skin-flicks" and erotic "art." Here morality comes into the esthetic field, and involves taste, judgment and discrimination. That the line is thin is shown by the disturbed reactions of ordinary people to such a "grand opera" as the German adaption by Richard Strauss (1864-1949), of the drama, in French, *Salome,* by the witty and brash Oscar Fingall O'Flahertie Wilde (1854-1900). Wilde was unpleasantly involved in homosexuality. He was representative of the Anglo-French "decadents" of the late 19th Century, including Charles Pierre Beaudelaire (1821-1867), whose *Les Fleurs du Mal* was a sensation in 1864, Aubrey Beardsley (1873-1898), the artist, and Stephane Mallarmé (1842-1898), the poet. These emotionally oriented rebels against conventional rationality were part of the existential movement, and greatly influenced our current irrationality.

A logically rational approach to sexual morality was made by Bertrand Russell (1892-1970), the great Cambridge logician and anti-metaphysical philosopher. In his *Marriage and Morals* (1932), he expounded matrimonial reforms in a manner advocating full mutual honesty in regard to sexual activity. Personal honesty with oneself and one's marriage partner, he felt, would resolve matrimonial problems.

The technological advances in contraceptives have greatly altered the morality of sexual activity, in that harm or social stigma to an innocent result of sex activity is greatly reduced. Unwanted pregnancies can now readily be avoided. Further evidence of the more rational approach to sexual morality is indicated by the gradual legalization of abortions in many parts of the world. Both contraception and abortion seem to be increasingly indicated in a world-wide effort to reduce overpopulation. For individual ethics, contraception and abortion involve the merits of wanted or unwanted children. In this instance, rational consideration of consequences would seem to be more conducive to satisfaction than to follow emotional feelings.

Sexual morality inevitably brings up the problems of jealousy, infidelity, and competitive rivalry. Here again, Bertrand Russell's arguments for honesty are pertinent - honesty with oneself, and with those with whom one may be sexually involved. Related is our whole social complex of interpersonal relations, with prestige, status, scandal, honor, trust, and even life itself, at stake. In spite of the awesome seriousness of all of this to the individuals concerned, it may be uneasily humorous to those outside. Persons who live in glass houses would be wise neither to laugh nor to throw stones, as intelligent people have long known.

It was Freud's genius to reveal the latent behavioral power

of repressed infantile sex fantasies in the attraction of siblings for parents of the opposite sex. Astonishing is the revelation of the antiquity of the recognition of these aspects of human life, as shown in the great *Oedipus Tyrannus* of Sophocles (496-405 B. C.), from which Freud derived his concept of the Oedipus complex. Analogous is the Elektra complex, again explored dramatically by Sophocles.

Social control of sexual activity, developing from Zoroaster, and St. Paul, through Calvanist puritanism, to Victorian hyprocrisy, was probably helpful in preparing for individual rationalism in sexual morality. The ethical problems remain to be solved by the rational understanding of individuals in regard to the wide ramifications of sex drives.

We are as yet greatly bothered by the question of sex education. Mary S. Calderone has brilliantly promoted a broad educational program on sex, by pamphlets, films and talks, through a volunteer organization, SIECUS (Sex Information and Education Council of U.S.), independent of government. Sex education of children by parents is usually complicated by the uneasiness both of parent and child, and teaching by an objective surrogate is often disliked both by parents and children. As my colleague, Ilza Veith observes, in an essay on "Education for Morality" (*Bull. Menninger Clin.*, 34:292-303, 1970), "We still have not resolved these issues."

In 1939-1941 I handled a volunteer no-credit course in sex education for some 2,600 students at the Berkeley campus of the University of California. It was an honest effort: I received no recompense and the students no credit. The course went smoothly as long as I talked in generalities, letting the students apply to themselves individually what they thought would fit. Further, I took the position that sex relationships are merely one aspect of interpersonal relations in general. Thus we discussed interpersonal relations carefully, and sex relations fell into place. World War II stopped the effort. My impression remains that the most satisfactory way to consider sex relations is as part of general, interpersonal relations. If these can be put in order, sex activity will tend to fall in line. Honesty in these matters, with oneself, and with others involved, will tend to maintain emotional and rational balance.

One of the most influential writers and speakers on moral aspects of sexual and moral customs is the great anthropologist Margaret Mead (1901-   ). Her objective descriptions of sex and social life in the South Pacific are popular with those wanting to show the relativity and wide differences in social and sexual behavior among different peoples. She has more recently devoted herself to current social problems in the USA. Her opinions are definite and precise and she enjoys expressing them.

The Freedom Ethic

Is individual freedom of action an acceptable ethic? Some people think so. This results in anarchy, as groups of people have found, from antiquity. Some social order is essential, apparently, unless all live as hermits. There isn't room enough for that. So, most pleas for individual freedom seem to be directed against government, even if the government is agreed upon by consent of the governed. Too often, however, that consent is forced. Coercion is part of the social pressure of the group on all of its members to conform to the standards established (hence "The Establishment") by presumed agreement of the members of the group. The alternative is to leave the group, or to be put out of it. Often violence enters, either with coercion, or in being put out.

Effective government is not simply tyranny, democracy, or anarchy. Dictatorships may be benign or bigoted, democracies may be irresponsible and oppressive to minorities, and anarchies may be conducive either to common weal or to common woe. So much depends on the individual personalities of those who are in the picture. Of the three major forces of government, democracy, whether Athenian town meeting, or Lockian representative, seems to be the most rational. In a democracy the emotional whims of individuals presumably are dampened by the statistical opinion in which all participate, again presumably with rational effort at a working compromise. On the contrary, both dictatorships or anarchic setups would seem to be more dependent on individual emotional conditions, oriented in a hedonistic manner. Democracy implies an operating social idealism. Utopias seem generally to be visioned as rational.

In any system of socially effective government a deep commitment to responsibility is implied. Indeed, it usually happens that the authority in a government is proportional to its responsibility. In a democracy, in order to be effective, however, it seems that the sense of responsibility must be shared by all: that is, the majority must show responsibility toward the welfare of the minority, if the effort is really to succeed; and the minority, likewise, if the general effort is to succeed, must show voluntary and responsible acquiescence to the will of the majority. Implied is the proposition that if it were to come to a physical showdown, the larger number would prevail. There is then, in a working democracy, a tacit agreement to go along cheerfully and responsibly with the will of the majority. There is, however, the continuing danger that the majority may become coercive and tyrannical. There is thus the responsibility on the majority to protect the minority from emotional waves and whims.

All of these aspects of government and politics are related to ethics. It will be recalled that Aristotle made his discussion of ethical theory as a preface to his discussion of politics. Morality plays a large role in the political success of individuals who are leaders in a democracy. Indeed it is often the basis on which judgment is passed by the citizens, whether in economic, humanitarian, or personal issues.

A growing number of dissenters are arguing, often violently, for a greater amount of individual freedom in individual action and opinion than the majority have countenanced. This seems to be the background of the "counter-culture," so well analyzed by Theodore Roszak (Doubleday Anchor Books, Garden City, New York, 1969, 303 pp.). The situation is complicated, however, by the growing technologies and bureaucracies, under which people are said to be increasingly dehumanized. This is part also of the existential revolt against rationality: people's sympathy is ever with Charlie Chaplin as he gets caught in the wheels of the machine.

Is it really the machines, or the people who set them up and use them - and for what purpose? It is pertinent that Norbert

Wiener (1894-1964), who had so much to do with applying feed-back principles to computer design, should have so clearly denounced *The Human Use of Human Beings, Summarized Essays on Cybernetics and Society* (Avon, New York, 1967, 288 pp.). A basic ethical question remains: how far do the ends to be sought justify the means for reaching them?

A large number of our young people want to answer this question for themselves, individually. They want no more of the stock clichés of the Establishment. These got us into bankruptcy, moral and financial, in a war few want: brought great poverty and squalor to great numbers; befouled our living places; exhausted our national resources; and brought tensions and violence into our midst. Slowly it is dawning that maybe a lot of this misery is caused by the simple fact that there are too many of us, the result largely of individual freedom to breed as we wish. Here, as always, individual freedom implies individual responsibility for the consequences of action.

The freedom ethic was first promulgated in recent times by that emotionally unstable, sexually promiscuous French writer, Jean-Jacques Rousseau (1712-1778). In his *Contrat Social* (Paris, 1762) he postulated the goodness of people in a state of nature, and that social contracts are associations to protect individuals, in which each, though united to all, would be self-governing and thus free. By surrendering oneself and one's possessions to the general goodwill, all contribute to the impartial welfare, free from private or sectarian interests. If one acts against the general will, one must be forced to be free, he claimed in his curious way. His slogan, "Liberty, Egality, Fraternity" became the watch word of the French Revolution. This started the romantic reaction against rationalism.

An influential practical application of Rousseau's nature philosophy was made by the Harvard thinker, the "hermit of Walden," Henry David Thoreau (1817-1862). His *Walden, or Life in the Woods* (Boston, 1854) described his gentle life in nature. He also wrote on and practiced civil disobedience when he considered a current legality, such as paying taxes, unjust. As in the later and more significant case of Mohandas Karamchand Ghandi (1869-1948), Thoreau denounced violence as ever being justified in seeking civil justice.

Gandhi was jailed twice (to Thoreau's once), for opposing the discriminatory legislation against the natives by the British in India. The mass effect of civil disobedience in India finally brought British compromise and then independence. The assassination of Gandhi by a Hindu fanatic made him a revered martyr, as in the case of Lincoln. Gandhi came to be considered a moral reformer who sought to free his countrymen from caste as well as from the snares of materialism. The Gandhian ethic, with its rather simple naturalistic religious background, is discussed by Benoy Gopal Ray (Navajivan, Ahmedabad, 1950, 59 pp.). He sought "spiritual perfection" in a life of continence in thought, speech and action. This was in full accord with the ancient Hindu tradition.

A clear plea for anarchy, on a rationalistic basis with individual moral responsibility was made by the Russian geographer, Peter Kropotkin (1842-1921). Although he espoused anarchy, he recognized the value of mutual aid in the evolution of social stability. His aim was a responsible individual freedom. He gave intellectual support to Vladimir Ilyich (Ulyanov) Lenin (1870-1924) in establishing the successful Russian Revolution of 1917.

Lenin's effort was directed toward the achievement of desired social reform (in Russia, the improvement in quality of living for the working masses) by revolution, with deliberate violence, if necessary, to force acquiescence to the new system of dominance of workers, as outlined by Karl Marx (1818-1883), the neurotic German exponent of communism, who did so much of his work in the British Museum. Lenin implemented Marx's theories, so that the general system which emerged is often called Marxist-Leninism. Lenin wrote extensively in support of his concept of "the dictatorship of the proletariat," and of the class-less society visioned by Marx and his collaborator, Friederich Engels (1820-1895) in their classic *Das Kapital* (1867).

How does the soviet system work? The word, "soviet," means a committee or group. There are soviets functioning everywhere in the USSR, in factories, stores, schools, apartments, sports, clinics, and libraries. They meet at various times. If small, they are almost like a townhall. A matter for decision may be brought apparently by anyone. The issue is debated vigorously from all standpoints. When everyone has expressed an opinion with the reasons therefor, the vote is taken. The decision is the expression of the majority, and that stands, until the issue may come up again. There is no responsibility on the majority to protect the interests or welfare of the minority; rather, it is the clear responsibility of the minority to accept the will of the majority and to abide cheerfully by it. A member of the group deviates from it at his or her peril. Bureaucrats in the USSR claim this to be real democracy. In general, this system seems to work well with general improvement in the welfare of the masses. It is supported by a vast and vested bureaucracy, which is little different from Czarist days.

The freedom ethic is attracting the interest of many of our youngsters and the alarm of their elders. Individual freedom in behavior is expressed in clothes, hair, arrogance, disregard for others, foul language, uncleanliness, slovenly living, emotionalism, drug abuse, mysticism, "dropping-out," anti-intellectualism, hatred for technology, contempt for science, oriental intuitism, far-out graphic art, rock music, religious parody, and sex. All the age-long traditions of Western cultural decency are flaunted by the freedom-seeking youngsters. Accustomed standards of etiquette, courtesy and politeness are contemptuously disregarded. It is significant of this counter-culture that one of its first large-scale public demonstrations at the University of California in Berkeley in 1964 should have been devoted to the attempt to make individuals free to use gutter language on any occasion, in particular the Anglo-Saxon four-letter words for common human excretory functions and sex activity.

It would seem that instead of the use of decent manners to lubricate the machinery of interpersonal relations, as is so characteristic of the "proper" Japanese and British, the counter-culture strives to employ abrasive conduct to wreck ordinary social intercourse. The excuse is that this crude behavior shows us as we really are. The counter-culture is thus a current aspect of existentialism, and the existentialist moralists are its heroes. Yet, it has had beneficial effects. It has revealed the extent of our deep ethical hypocrisies. It has exposed the crassness of competitive exploitation of masses of people by the greedy extensions of technology. And it has raised the searching questions of values in warfare and in peaceful welfare. It has brought us to a crisis in moral valuation.

The basic inconsistency of the counter-culture lies in its attempted justification of violence in order to achieve its ends of individual freedom. Here the concept of individual freedom shows no trace of responsibility to anyone or anything except oneself. Freedom thus becomes individual license to do anything, with total anarchy resulting.

One of the major prophets of the counter-culture, Herbert Marcuse (1898-   ) of the University of California, San Diego, has written specifically urging violence in social revolution in order to get what is wanted ("Ethics and Revolution," in *Ethics and Society,* R. T. de George, ed., Doubleday Anchor, Garden City, New York, 1966, pp. 133-147). He concludes that "the end justifies the means, namely, if they demonstrably serve human progress in freedom." He goes on, echoing Lenin, "the end must be operative in the repressive means for attaining the end. But no matter how rational, how necessary, how liberating - revolution involves violence." This is the kind of talk which resulted in Angela Davis, and the death of the Marin County judge and the court intruders who took him hostage.

Marcuse's arguments for this point of view are shot full of dubious assumptions, non-sequitors, and a peculiar Germanic frustrated emotionalism. His *One-Dimensional Man* (Beacon Press, Boston, 1964, 260 pp.) offers the same general critique of social morality in philosophical jargonese. With Marcuse, moral formulations and ethical theories go out of the window: human welfare, supposedly both individual and social, is to be ameliorated only by violent revolution, with the rebels enforcing their victory by further violence.

Thus the millenia of cultural evolution and moral formulation for satisfying interpersonal relations, for individual and social welfare, are negated in a nihilism in which only chaos remains. Individual freedom has long since disappeared from the ends sought by Marcuse. Of responsibility in connection with that freedom, not even a memory is left.

Apparently Marcuse wants to start all over again in the long way up from infantile ethical formulation to the inevitable compromises that come with maturity, which seek to harmonize the satisfactions of individuals with the general welfare of the societies to which they belong. Marcuse talks as if he'd like to be a Big Boss, and an irresponsible one at that. There is a place for a freedom ethic, but it is not likely to be where Marcuse and the neo-existentialists want it to be. The survival aspects of biological (which includes sociological) adaption are against them.

The Ethic of a New Humanism

Many years before Charles Perry Snow (1905-   ), the English science novelist, popularized the gap between the two cultures of rational science and technology on the one hand and of emotional intuitive art and the humanities on the other, George Alfred Leon Sarton (1884-1956), the Belgian mathematician, was already trying to close it. His attempt was largely to humanize science and technology by revealing their fascinating history. Showing that scientific endeavor has given us our chief verifiable knowledge of ourselves and of our environment, he has indicated clearly our individual and social responsibility to apply this knowledge carefully to the long range benefit of ourselves and of the world we inhabit.

An indefatigable scholar, Sarton established the history of science as an independent intellectual discipline. To this end he founded and edited *Isis* in 1913. A quarterly journal, now in its 63rd volume, it is famed for its comprehensive critical bibliography of historical writings about science. In 1927 he founded and edited *Osiris,* a medium for the publication of monographs on the history of science. Fleeing from the Germans in World War I, he came to the USA with his wife and infant daughter, May, who is now a distinguished poet and novelist. May Sarton has written delightful accounts of her parents for *The New Yorker.*

Sarton completed three volumes of a monumental *Introduction to the History of Science* (Carnegie Institution Washington, D. C., 1927-1948), and wrote many books, essays and articles on various topics related to the ever-fascinating way by which dedicated people over the ages have added to our ever-increasing understanding of ourselves and of our environment. In all of these, there always has been a solid foundation of ethical purpose, usually expressed in some aspect of social idealism. Sarton was a brilliant teacher. His lectures and writings were vibrant with his cheerful sincerity. For all of this he was widely honored at home, where he worked at Harvard, and abroad. A talented linguist, he showed his sincerity and skill by learning Arabic, so that he might properly evaluate the many almost unrecognized scientific achievements of the Muslims.

Sarton thought that a crucial problem of our time is how to obtain the benefits of social unity without losing the values of individual responsible freedom. He sought to accomplish this by trying to unify, in a common motivation, all people of "goodwill." He points out that people of goodwill, trying to increase "our treasures of charity, beauty, justice and truth" are struggling in the same direction, but not always at the same time. Thus their efforts may separately be defeated by the ever-present ruthless human brutes who fatten themselves at the expense of their neighbors. Sarton's essay on unification of good-will (*Isis,* 211-215, 1937) summarizes his ethical opinions forcefully. My wife and I reprinted it as a holiday greeting for our friends in 1937.

Social evils, said Sarton, are diseases. Like actual physical diseases, they can only be treated when they have been accurately diagnosed, and their causes revealed. People do not enjoy the revelation of dishonesty, greed, cruelty, atrocity, or crass exploitation any more than they want to see ugly wounds or ulcerations. Yet this revelation is a necessary condition for effective therapy. So, we must seek the causes for our social ills, and expose those individuals responsible for them. This is a particular example of the general principle of continuing to search for the truth about ourselves and about the world we live in. Further, this search for this truth, if it is to be effective, must be free, unencumbered by bias, prejudice, fear, or outside coercion.

Sarton recognized the acceleration of scientific knowledge and the ever-increasing applications of it in technologies polarized toward war and peace. A major problem for our time is how to try to turn the balance toward peace, and all that is implied therein. Sarton died before technological advances, such as sophisticated computers, were being made that may aid us in turning away from war and moving toward a stable peace. It is important to realize that scientific enterprise is truly without national boundaries, so that similar technologies are now characteristic of even such great opposing powers as the USA, USSR and China. It is the mutual possession of nuclear power, computer and world scanning communication, that now deters flagrant aggression. Slowly we are learning to work together, as in the control of disease, and the exploration of Antartica or space.

One of the most rational of current ethical movements is the one called "Humanism." This is an educational effort, in which people are viewed as evolutionary and historical products of our world. It acknowledges no supernatural processes or purposes. It has been especially furthered and supported by Edwin H. Wilson, of Yellow Springs, Ohio, Corliss Lamont of Columbia University, New York City, and Paul Kurtz of the University of Buffalo. Many liberal intellectuals write for *The Humanist,* and publish under its auspices, such as Sidney Hook of New York University. In addition to editing *The Humanist* (now in its 33rd year), Paul Kurtz has edited *Moral Problems in Contemporary Society: Essays in Humanistic Ethics* (Prentice-Hall, Englewood Cliffs, New Jersey, 1969, 301 pp.). This contains eighteen perceptive analyses of various aspects of the humanistic effort, all of them basically optimistic over control of emotion, and over our ability to develop ourselves and our world in a way that is conducive to our long-range welfare, individual happiness and social peace.

Suddenly we have become aware of a gigantic threat to us all. We have grown so rapidly and abundantly that we are threatening our own destruction by exhausting our natural resources; by polluting our airs and waters to the point of death; by starving through impossibility of a linear growing food supply to keep pace with an exponentially growing population, and compounding our individual and social tensions and frustrations by our urban crowding. The Malthusian prophecies are coming true. This becomes a matter of world dynamics. Jay Wright Forrester (1918-   ) of the famed Massachusetts Institute of Technology, is using computerized analyses in the exploration of "systems dynamics." In one of these he has devised a dynamic model which interrelates population, capital investment, geographical space, natural resources, pollution, and food production at world levels. This operates with various feedback loops. The findings, in some instances, are ominous, and in some, unexpected.

Agreeing with the conclusions of the Club of Rome's report, *The Limits to Growth* (Universe Books, New York, 1972, 205 pp.), Forrester (*Bull. Amer. Acad. Arts & Sciences,* 25:No. 7, April, 1972) finds that however the variables are altered in his systems dynamics model, the computer analyses point toward the necessity of stopping growth, if we could avoid disaster, from revolution, genocide, violence or war. We can yet attain equilibrium, but the transition from a basic philosophy of growth to one of equilibrium will be fraught with trauma, especially to social values. However, this is part of the long lesson of biological evolution, which we have by no means learned. Only those living things which can adapt to changing environments can survive. One would think that our brains would help us.

In his *Science and Survival* (Ballantine Books, New York, 1970, 177 pp.), Barry Commoner, the eminent St. Louis biologist, shows in specific detail how our ruination of our environment can all too quickly bring disaster upon us. He well emphasizes the interrelations of all living processes in the closed system of our world, in which disturbance in one factor in the equilibrium must bring adjustments or compensations throughout the whole, if the balance is to survive. We are now on the precarious edge of general disaster from overpopulation and its attending ills of tensions, technological breakdowns, pollution of airs and water, and exhaustion of natural resources.

A difficulty always with us, is that we all want change for the better, in the short time of our own individual lives, not being willing to acknowledge that natural evolutionary processes in human societies take generations. We can, however, all of us, begin at once to get over a hankering to grow bigger, whether physically, in business or in corporations, in cities, in armaments, in schools, or in numbers of people in a family or nation, or in the world. If we are to survive we must learn to accept equilibrium as preferable to growth. This does not mean stopping intellectual and moral growth, but rather using our intelligence to get satisfactions in equilibrium, especially in emotional, financial, and prestige affairs. Sarton's plea for good-willed co-operation could help.

The Relativistic Ethic: Situationalism

Great scientific advances have many consequences, often on ethical theory. Newton's demonstration of law and order in the universe of the stars fired people on earth, powerful thinkers often, such as Kant, who sought to find ways to make law and order supreme among us humans. Darwin's demonstration of selective and adaptive powers in living things conducive to survival was reflected in ethical theory from Spencer on to the present. Einstein's demonstration of relativity in the physical world has made absolutes questionable and potentially untenable, in law, in morals, and in religions. The clearest exposition of a relativistic ethic so far advanced is that by Joseph Francis Fletcher III (1905-   ), wise and witty scholar of the Theological School in Cambridge, Massachusetts. His ideas are embodied in *Situation Ethics: The New Morality* (Westminster Press, Philadelphia, 1966, 176 pp.). This has become quite a classic. It was amplified by a volume entitled *Moral Responsibility: Situation Ethics at Work* (Westminster Press, Philadelphia, 1967, 256 pp.). This gives practical applications in relation to sexual activity, fertility control, the right of a person to die, business management, wealth, and stewardship.

Fletcher concludes his well-documented study by claiming that the theological virtues of faith, hope and agapic love have the most fundamental and practical importance for satisfying living in a mass society. The virtue of agapic love, he thinks, can be enough to cope effectively with any situation. Since the actual situations which one encounters in life are never exactly the same, and usually similar only in part, one cannot rely on any single ethical theory, except that of responsible agapic love, in approaching them. One's behavior then, in deciding what to do, when the moral factors entering there-in are considered, depends on the situation, and on one's responsible analysis of it and of the consequences of one's actions or opinions in regard to it.

It is not quite this simple. Fletcher says there are only three approaches possible in making moral decisions: (1) a legalistic; (2) its extreme opposite in a lawless or unprincipled way, and (3) somewhere between, a situational. He goes on to analyze these approaches to moral decisions chiefly from an historical basis in Judeo-Christian ethics. With legalism, he says, one comes to moral decisions burdened with "a whole apparatus of prefabricated rules and regulations." Under this way, the letter of the rules often dominates over their spirit, and they tend to become contradictory as they multiply. All Western religious traditions have been legalistic. The extreme opposite, reaching moral decisions on the spur of the moment, with no guiding princple, bring ethical anarchy. In the middle way of situation ethics, agapic love is the guiding principle. With situational ethics, one realizes the relativity of the particular situation with which one is concerned, and seeks a solution, with responsible regard for consequences, in accordance with the influence of agapic love in bringing goodwilled agreement.

Fletcher's point of view makes for specific case orientation. Indeed, his ethical interests seem to have crystallized first in relation to the real ethical problems of medical practice, such as abortion, contraception, euthanasia, the right of a patient to know the truth, or to die, and human experimentation. His study, *Morals and Medicine* (Princeton University Press, 1954, 306 pp.), was largely case presentations, but it focused attention on the problems of genuine medical ethics. These had been neglected for decades by organized medical societies, which had, instead, emphasized the expediencies of etiquette.

So, Fletcher uses case histories to illustrate his ethical position. Often he leaves the solution to the reader, confident apparently that agapic love will show the way. Fletcher's implication of a religious background of agapic love for responsible ethical judgment echoes Paul Tillich (*Morality and Beyond,* Harper, New York, 1963, 101 pp.).

Fletcher's situation ethics emphasizes individual free responsibility, based on agapic love, in making any moral judgment. This can rid us of the burden of rigid, archaic rules and codes of conduct. Each of us must decide for ourselves what is "right" in any particular situation, provided that we rely on the guidance of agapic love. From this it seems to follow that any act, sexual, political, even lying, theft, adultery, or murder, could be the right and proper one, if the circumstances of the situation would justify it. However, individual responsibility remains paramount. Fletcher says, "Responsibility means a free and critical conformity to the facts, first of all - the shifting patterns of situations - and then to the unchanging single norm or boss principle of loving concern for persons and the social balance."

The Ethic of *NOPSIR:* Naturally Operating Principle of Survival of Interpersonal Relationships

The discussion so far has been concerned with various answers over the centuries to the basic questions which bother us all, occasionally in consciousness, usually subconscious, *What are we living for?, What motivates us? What are our purposes and goals, in general or in particular? What guides our conduct?, What shapes our opinions about ourselves and other people?.* The answers to these questions are the various ethical theories or moral formulations which have been proposed over millenia, from the Big Boss idea, to responsible agapic love. Two of the original questions have so far been only vaguely touched upon. These are: what governs our interpersonal relations, and what determines our moods and behavior? Both imply something of a deterministic, materialistic, strictly rational point of view.

These questions are framed in the light of the remarkable rationalistic biological manifesto of 1847 of three great German precisionistic physiologists, all keen young thinkers, Karl Friedrich Wilhelm Ludwig (1816-1895), Hermann von Helmholtz (1821-1894), and Emil Du Bois-Reymond (1818-1896). They all contributed greatly to our understanding of the complex way in which our bodies function, and they were deeply imbued with the scientific spirit of their time. They united in stating flatly and categorically, as an article of faith, that all living processes, including human consciousness, are explainable in terms of physics and chemistry.

This came at the same time as the better known manifesto of Karl Marx (1818-1883) and Friederich Engels (1820-1895) to the effect that all history and economics are explainable in materialistic terms. The biological manifesto was taken to Russia by Ivan Michailovich Sechenov (1829-1905), a liberal pupil of Ludwig, who demonstrated the general inhibitory influence of the later cortex of brains on the earlier developed parts of the nervous systems. The Marxian ideas were implemented in Russia by Lenin. The two manifestos induced the materialistic cast so characteristic of thought in the USSR.

The question of what governs our interpersonal relations arose with me on a specific occasion in the early autumn of 1939. My wife, Elisabeth, and I had a little redwood retreat on the San Lorenzo River in the Santa Cruz mountains. There we would go for weekends of woodsy play with our two boys. We usually asked the laboratory workers to join us for a Sunday seminar. The California coast redwoods grow in circles around some long-gone stump. We arranged one of these circles with benches, and a blackboard on a tree trunk, and we had as comfortable a seminar setting as anyone would want.

On one of these weekends in 1939, the American Association for the Advancement of Science was meeting at Stanford, a few miles over the hills to the east. We asked some friends to join us: Edwin Grant Conklin (1863-1952), Professor of Biology at Princeton, my revered teacher; Olaf Larsell

(1886-1966), Professor of Neuro-anatomy at the University of Oregon, who had been one of my teachers at Wisconsin; and Charles Judson Herrick (1868-1960), distinguished Professor of Neurophysiology at the University of Chicago. We had a discussion of recent French philosophy by Charles Gurchot, and of recent German philosophy by the studious medical moralist, Otto Guttentag, both members of our laboratory group. Professor Conklin, who was interested in the possible relations of science and ethics, raised the question as to whether or not we might be able to formulate a naturally operating biological principle which would have ethical significance.

We mulled this over for a while, and decided to try to frame it in reference to Darwinian survival factors. We further agreed to try to have it apply to interpersonal relations. In such relationships of people with each other we thought the hub of ethical problems is to be found. We wanted an emotionally neutral statement, a descriptive formulation of what goes on in human relationships whether we like it or not, or even whether or not we are aware of it. We wanted it to be something like the principle of gravity!

Gradually we induced from the plethora of our experience this statement: *The probability of survival of a relationship between individuals or groups of individuals increases with the extent to which that relationship is mutually satisfying.* We realized that we were properly scientific and statistical by opening with "probability." We applied Darwinian survival factors to relationships between people, stressing their mutuality. We were a bit troubled about the sense of satisfaction, but we felt we had included a potent motivation. We amused ourselves by considering some of the collaries to our statement. It seemed to imply something of the "Golden Rule.": if one were in a satisfying relationship with someone else, then there would seem to be an obligation to try to make that relationship as satisfying to the other as to oneself, if the relationship were to last.

The usual relationships that might be involved are wife and husband; parent and child; sisters and brothers; lover and beloved; homosexual and homosexual; business man and

competitor; even enemy and enemy; teacher and pupil; fore-
man and worker; master and slave; employer and employee;
capitalists and laborers; town and town; city and city; state
and state; nation and nation. The interpersonal relationships
in these various situations seem always to be in flux, ever
seeking greater stability and equilibrium in mutual satisfaction. This seems to apply even in situations involving sadism
and masochism, or any aspect of dominance and submission.
The interpersonal relationship might even involve hatred and
violence, if that were mutually satisfying. Yet, the sense of
satisfaction is basically one of relaxation, and mutual satisfaction as an interpersonal relationship would seem to tend more
toward an agapic understanding than otherwise.

The statement does seem to embody a naturally operating
principle. This principle does operate apparently, whether we
like it or not, or even whether or not we are aware of it. Thus it
is psychologically similar to the principle of gravity. In the
case of gravity, it has benefited us greatly to be aware of it and
to utilize it to our advantage. Perhaps this would be the case
were we to be fully aware at all times, in our interpersonal
relations, that, if we wish them to survive, we must strive to
make them as satisfying to others involved as to ourselves.

An account of this naturally operating principle of survival
of interpersonal relations has been published on many occasions. It was first given at the Cleveland meeting of the
American Association for the Advancement of Science in
1944. It was published in three slightly varying forms (*Sci.
Month.*, 60:245-253, 1945; *Proc. Texas Philosoph. Soc.*,
Dallas, 1945; *Studies and Essays in the History of Science and
Culture Offered in Homage to George Sarton,* Schuman, New
York, 1946, pp. 261-275). This effort grew from my reaction
to a discussion on science and ethics which I had arranged for
the 1940 Philadelphia meeting of the American Association
for the Advancement of Science. This in turn came from
thought resulting in an essay, "Science Implies Freedom,"
which was privately printed in 1939, and published later in
Studies in the History of Culture (Amer. Council Learned
Soc., Menasha, Wisconsin, 1942, 310-320).

My *Scientific Monthly* article on "ethicogenesis" inspired a spirited and carefully argued reply from Patrick Romanell, then Professor of Philosophy at Wells College, Aurora, New York, and a devoted pupil of William Pepperell Montagu (1873-1953), long-time Professor of Philosophy at Columbia University, New York City. Doctor Romanell properly took me to task for my rather sophomoric disdain for metaphysics. I had confused the imaginative but rationally controlled surmises of metaphysical contemplation with explanations and speculations about ourselves and our environment which bring in supernatural or other irrational considerations. I was inclined to dismiss metaphysics, as I witnessed its status in philosophy, as wishful thinking about and yearning for asymptotic ideals. Doctor Romanell assured me that metaphysics is rather the consideration in ethics of what may be possible, in human relations, for people to find agreeable as moral ideals. I'm right on with this.

When Doctor Romanell's essay, "A Philosopher's Reply To a Scientist's Ethic" appeared (*Sci. Monthly.,* 61:293-306, 1945), I corresponded with him, and eventually asked him to join our effort at the University of Texas Medical Branch in Galveston. This he did, and our debates continued. Finally, they were collected in a nicely printed little volume, *Can We Agree?* (University of Texas Press, Austin, 1950, xiv 110 pp.). Later Doctor Romanell continued his philosophical studies at the University of Texas, El Paso, where he became an authority on recent Italian and Latin-American philosophy. He brought sharp logical critique to my thesis, and later developed a naturalistic philosophy of his own.

The statement induced by Conklin, Herrick, Larsell, Gurchot, Guttentag, and me, *the probability of survival of a relationship between humans or groups of humans increases with extent to which that relationship is mutually satisfying,* was subjected to some analysis. It seemed that we had succeeded in formulating an objective scientific principle, operative ethically, but free from metaphysical implications. The statement could be phrased, "the more a relationship between people is mutually satisfying, the longer it tends to last," or more carefully, *"Behavior patterns between individ-*

ual persons or groups of people tend to become adjusted (by trial and miss) toward those which yield the greatest mutual satisfaction." This latter phraseology would be in accord with feedback control mechanisms of adjustments to stress in any closed system.

Though inducible from the myriad of examples that could be cited, the statement nevertheless has a touch of the axiomatic about it, even if it is not tautological. Specific case histories of behavior patterns between particular individuals, and factors involved in their constancy or change, are to be found especially in psychiatric literature. There are many historical examples of gradual adjustments toward more mutually satisfying (and mutually beneficial) behavior patterns between groups of people. Often these adjustments have been made under the pressure of war. It seems now, in many instances, that we are learning to utilize more peaceful means to obtain the satisfying ends we all want.

What is the meaning of "satisfaction" about which we've been talking? We did not really know much about it in a demonstrable scientific way until quite recently. Neurophysiological studies on all kinds of animals, and in various widely scattered scientific institutions, from the USSR, to India, to many other centers, and to the USA, are bringing agreement on factors that seem to determine our moods and behavior, and on their cyclic operations which give us our conditionable sense of satisfaction. Evidence is accumulating that mood and behavior, in large part, are regulated by the cyclic activity of cell centers in the limbic system and hypothalamic areas of our brain stems. The limbic system is that great relay complex of neurons, through which sensory input is channeled to the mid - and fore-brain, and through which motor output is directed to muscles and glands. It is a very primitive part of our central nervous system.

As summarized so neatly by Paul D. MacLean of the National Institute of Mental Health at Bethesda, Maryland (*The Central Nervous System and Behavior, Trans. 2nd Conf.*, 1959, Josiah Macy, Jr., Foundation, New York City, pp. 51-118; *Amer. J. Med.*, 25:611-626, 1958), two major cell centers are involved. These were implicated by J. W. Papez (1883-1958), in mechanisms of emotion (*Arch. Neurol. & Psychiat.,* 38:725-743, 1937), and had been physiologically implied by Nobelatent Walter Bradford Cannon (1871-1945) in his concept of homeostasis (*The Wisdom of the Body,* W. W. Norton, New York, 1939, 333 pp.; *Bodily Changes in Pain, Hunger, Fear and Rage,* Harper, New York, 404 pp.).

Of these two limbic system, or "visceral brain," cell centers, one has to do with self-preservation, and controls the feeling of hunger and the search for, and intake of food. The other has to do with species preservation and is involved in the drive for sex. A greatly simplified explanation of their probable mechanism of action follows. It is assuredly a very complex mechanism, varying greatly in detail between different people.

Food intake centers seem to be regulated by a sort of "glucostat." When the energy-giving carbohydrates in these cells diminish, as in low blood sugar, the "stat" goes on and the cells become active. Their activity goes along with outpouring of epinephrine from the adrenal medulla, and the muscles gradually tense, blood pressure rises, and the individual is oriented toward a search for food. Individuals when hungry are aggressive. It matters not whether one is in jungle primitivism, or in the most sophisticated society, every six hours or so one scrounges after food. When ingested, the food is digested in the alimentary tract, its components get into the metabolic cycle of the liver, the blood sugar rises, the energy producing compounds in the cells of the food-intake centers in the limbic system increase, and the "glucostat" shuts off. There is muscular relaxation, lowering of blood pressure, a feeling of comfort and contentment, repose, and a drowsiness inviting sleep. This is the feeling of satisfaction. It is what we live for.

It is important to realize that this desirable feeling is strongly conditionable in accordance with the classic process outlined so well by Ivan Petrovich Pavlov (1849-1936). This conditioning starts with most of us at our first meal at our mother's breast. The bodily warmth and comfort, the contented muscular relaxation, the drowsiness, are all part of the feeling of satisfaction which we all subconsciously seek. Our conditioning varies for all of us as we mature. We learn that we can get this same good feeling of satisfaction from the successful pursuit of many other goals in addition to food. These goals may range from praise and fame, to artistic or intellectual achievement, to money, prestige and power. In any case, achievement of what we want, either in particular or in general, is followed by this same pleasing feeling of satisfaction. When we are on the hunt for our goals, we are tense, aggressive, impatient, intolerant, often mean. When we get them, we are relaxed, comfortable, agreeable, tolerant, often generous, and satisfied with ourselves and our environment. Wisely our fund-raisers or other goal seekers know how to get their guests well fed before putting the bite on them. The art of seduction seems to be to get the seducee satisfied, in some way, first.

When we start to mature, the sex drive cells begin to become cyclically active. In these cells a different kind of mechanism seems to be involved. This depends on the gradual metabolic build-up in these cells of many biogenic amines, such as epinephrine, nor-epinephrine, 5-hydroxytryptamine (serotonin), dopamine, acetylcholine, and probably many others, as well as many other ionizable organic compounds, and the inorganic ions of positively charged sodium, potassium, magnesium and calcium, and the negatively charged ions of chloride, sulphate, phosphate, and others.

As the metabolic build-up goes on, the positively charged ions seem to migrate toward the cell boundaries or interfaces, while the negatively charged ions congregate in the interior of the cell. The cells in the sex-drive center thus become polarized, or charged, and scientific language coincides with popular expression. As the polarization of the cells in these sex-drive centers increases, the individual is increasingly oriented toward a sex object, and the sex drive is on. The impulses from the cells go, by the vast nerve and chemical pathways, to all part of the body. The muscles become tense, respiration quickens, blood-pressure increases, sensory input to the fore-brain increases, and stimulates release of memory bundles which give anticipatory and directive guidance to overall activity. These effects increase in intensity, as the sexual action proceeds, until the climax is reached and orgasm occurs. Sudden depolarization of the cells in the sex-drive center occurs, and there follows muscular relaxation, reduced respiration and blood pressure, an overall feeling of contentment and satisfaction, repose and often the desire to sleep.

It should be noted that, as far as the activity of the cells in the sex-drive centers is concerned, it makes no difference whether the sex activity resulting therefrom is hetero-, homo, or auto. In a frank materialistic interpretation, then, what becomes of our centuries of ethical theory and social mores based on a puritanical notion of the sinfulness of sexual activity except for procreation? That they are conditional is clear, but this does not mitigate against their effectiveness.

There are many consequences, it seems, from the feeling of satisfaction resulting from the cyclic activities of the food-intake cell centers for self-preservation and of the sex-drive limbic cell centers for species preservation. The sex-drive cell-centers do not show as relatively regular cycles as the food-intake centers. They are more intensely activated in young maturity than in older people. The feeling of satisfaction is withheld, of course, if the drives are not carried through, either for food or for sex. Since these limbic system cell-centers seem to be close anatomically, there may be overlapping activity, and often compensation. An inadequate sex-drive release often is made up, as it were, by overeating. Conversely, it is not mere coincidence that semi-starved peoples have the highest birth-rates.

The drive for the mood of satisfaction, no matter to what it may be conditioned, is a powerful one. That warm comfortable relaxed sleepy feeling of satisfaction, after the drive to achieve it has succeeded, does seem to be the answer to that basic question, which all of our ethical theories have tried to answer, *"What are we living for?"* The operation of the limbic system cell centers for food-intake and self-preservation, and of sex-drive and species-preservation seems also to determine fundamentally our moods and behavior, no matter how conditioned.

A serious difficulty, however, has arisen over drugs. If drugs are found, as they are, on individual trial, to give the relaxed feeling of conditioned satisfaction, such drugs will be sought, used, and often misused. Drug absue often results from ignorance or indifference to the harm such misuse may cause. Yet too often drug abuse stems from the pathetic need to get some degree of satisfaction, at whatever cost. The mood of dissastifaction, while very unpleasant, is very powerful also. People seek to get away from it in many ways, including overeating, sexual excess and drugs.

There develops in most people a strong psychodynamism in relation to dissatisfaction, which if unrestrained may bring disaster, individually and socially. A state of continual satisfaction would seem to be boring beyond endurance. Such a condition is precluded in a healthy person by the cyclic metabolic activity of the limbic-system cell-centers for self- and species-preservation. Depending, then, on what the hunger- and sex-drives are conditioned to, either in general or in some particular, dissatisfaction seems to be an ever present lurking and leering evil. One usually has, at least subconsciously, the sneaky suspicion that what is so urgently wanted may not be had.

When an individual realizes that there is a *possibility* of not getting the satisfaction which may be desired in connection with any specific goal or with any purpose in general, there may come a feeling of anxiety. If not too great, this may aid in further endeavor to achieve the desired goal. On the other hand, if the situation goes on to the realization of the *probability* of failing to get the satisfaction desired, there comes frustration.

At this point in the psychodynamism of dissatisfaction, a peculiar psychological factor often intervenes. A frustrated person usually focusses the frustration upon some other person, usually near and often dear. This innocent individual on whom frustration is focussed, becomes the object of resentment, hostility and antagonism. With increasing reinforcement and buildup of the psychological factors involved, the focusing of frustration may go on to hatred, and thus to vengeance. The mood may blow off in anger.

An outsider witnessing the focusing of frustration may aid in clearing the situation by helping the frustrated person to discharge the anger by verbal or muscular exercise. Games, such as golf, often provide such an outlet. If, however, the angry frustrated mood is contained and the psychological reinforcement, real or imagined, continues, the result may be totally unpredictable, appearing as blind rage, with homicide or suicide as the consequence.

This focusing of frustration may occur between parents and children, between marriage partners, between teachers and students, between workmen and bosses, between sick patients in a hospital and anyone of the attending health personnel, between rivals in politics, business or love, between haves and have-nots, or in any hierarchal system, whether ecclesiastical, industrial or political. Sometimes, as in political assassination, it is directed against a surrogate father, or Big Boss.

Often the person against whom frustration is focused is thought "to stand in the way" of getting whatever satisfaction is being sought. When the resentment against such a one is great, the feeling of revenge may come along. This seems to be a primitive perversion of the idea of justice - "getting even" with somebody who is thought deliberately to have prevented the getting of the satisfaction craved. Vengeance thus becomes itself a goal, from the attainment of which satisfaction is to be derived. Duelling, as a ritualized form of interpersonal behavior, seems to show characteristics of this sort.

Many drugs, over the course of centuries, have been found to alter mood and behavior. Many of those commonly used, especially alcoholic beverages, directly produce muscular relaxation, lowering of blood pressure, relief from mental tension, anxiety, and frustration and thus give the conditioned feeling of satisfaction and prevent the progress of the psychodynamism of dissatisfaction.

Drugs, however, perform no miracles. They can merely make living material do relatively more or less what it is already capable of doing. The active agent in any drug, natural, crude, or synthetic, is chemical. Thus the biological activity of any drug occurs at a molecular level where the molecules of the drug interact with the molecules of the living material. Although drug action starts at a molecular level, it moves in a domino manner to subcellular units, then to cells, to organs and tissues, to individuals, to groups of individuals, and to environments.

The intensity of drug action is dependent on several factors: (1) the dosage, or mass of chemical per mass of living material; (2) the ratio of the rate of absorption of the drug into, and the rate of its removal from the living material; (3) the physico-chemical properties of the drug (which determine the interaction of its molecules with the molecules of living material; and (4) the peculiar specific characteristics of the living material under consideration. This last factor varies enormously. It cannot be accurately estimated and is largely up to the attending physician's judgment. It is dependent on age, sex, metabolic state, allergic sensitivities, pathological condition and homeostatic situation.

Because of this variation, there is wide difference in the action of the same dose of the same drug in different individuals. Gaussian distribution occurs, with some people showing scarcely any effect from the same dose of the same drug which may cause a very great effect, even death, in others. Most of us, fortunately, fall in between. There is greater variation among people in their responses to repeated administration than to a single dose. In general, intravenous injection of a dose of a drug in solution will give a much greater wallop than that same dose given by mouth. Some people seem to want this sort of a bang when they are abusively self-medicating with potent drugs such as heroin or the amphetamines. The effect is described by them as an ecstatic orgasm.

Drugs acting on the brain and central nervous system are of three kinds: (1) those which stimulate and increase brain and central nervous system activity; (2) those which depress this activity; and (3) those which distort it. Among the stimulants to the central nervous system, which are commonly abused, are cocaine, the amphetamines, and caffeine, in order of potency. These increase muscle tension, promote alertness, and give a feeling of being able to surmount difficulties in a generally unpleasant environment, by increasing the sense of power. They also make one more sensitive to one's environment.

Drugs which depress the brain and central nervous system are the general anesthetics, the opiates (including morphine and heroin), the barbitals, chloral, alcoholic beverages, and even aspirin. They promote muscular relaxation and sleep, and allay pain. The opiates, barbitals, chloral and the alcoholic beverages especially give a feeling of relaxed and comfortable well-being, and this feeling of conditioned satisfaction is what is sought by people who are frustrated in the midst of an unsatisfying and unpleasant environment.

The drugs causing distortion of brain activity are the hallucinating agents, such as mescaline (from peyote), psilocybin (from hallucinating mushrooms), and the notorious synthetic LSD (lysergic saure or acid diethylamide), which was derived from ergot. Cannabis, hemp, or marijuana, does not really come into any of the above three classes. It is a mild euphoric, causing some muscular relaxation, a feeling of comfort, with reduced vision, reduced interest in or attentiveness to the surroundings, but with an increased sense of touch. The tranquilizers, such as meprobamate, are very mild central nervous system depressants. Some, such as reserpine, pull ionizable amines out of the cells of the brain stem, thus depolarizing them and reducing their activity. Such recently popular drugs as "valium" and "librium" are synthetic chlordiazepoxides, chemically, and very mild muscle relaxants and tranquilizers.

The effect of alcoholic beverages on mood and behavior are especially interesting, since there is such extensive use of them, and has been since antiquity. They depress brain function progressively downwards, from the higher cortical centers of perception, cognition, and learned conformity to social norms, to the mid-brain areas for muscular control, and in large amounts to the medullary cell centers regulating vital functions. An ancient saying is "in vino veritas," suggesting the long recognized tendency of alcoholic beverages to reveal the underlying personality traits of the imbiber.

In some people with chronic dissatisfaction from suppressed frustration, alcoholic beverages may cause aggressive and pugnacious behavior. On the other hand, in persons with reasonably satisfying adjustments to living, alcoholic beverages may induce relaxed and cheerful contentment, albeit with loquaciousness. Some of these reactions show area character-istics, as with the pugnaciousness of the drunken Irishman, the arrogance of the drunken Prussian, the selfishness of the tipsy American, or the sentimentality of the boozy Bavarian.

All mood-altering drugs are capable of being abused. In the continual search for satisfaction, many people try many different kinds of drugs and usually find the ones which are thought to be suited to their individual situations. Many are addictive. The opiates, in particular, cause physical dependen-cy. Social regulation by prohibition or police is not effective, but cause racketeering and crime. Where there is profit to be made by supplying what is prohibited or difficult to get, racketeering and corruption tend to flourish. One would be expected to think that we would learn, from our failures, to stop trying by prohibition to control what people may want. Education may help. But this is a long slow process. The use of alcoholic beverages and hemp have been beneficial in some instances and harmful in others, for thousands of years, but we still have their problems with us.

At the 1970 Chicago meeting of the American Association for the Advancement of Science, there was a three-day session with 28 discussions on mood, behavior and drugs (*Science,* 170:559-560, Oct. 30, 1970). There was vigorous debate, and general agreement on scientific aspects of the problem, but little on satisfactory social control of drug abuse. This problem remains under political scrutiny with international ramifications.

The factors regulating interpersonal relations, and our moods and behavior are beginning to be rationally explored. It seems possible to formulate a naturally operating principle regulating the survival of interpersonal relations: the probabil-ity of survival of interpersonal relations between individuals or groups of individuals increases with the extent to which such relationships are mutually satisfying. The psychological fac-tors involved in the feeling of satisfaction are of paramount importance. This feeling of satisfaction is what we are living for.

Practical Applications of Ethical Theory

Whatever I want to do is either
illegal, immoral or fattening.

-Popular saying in the USA.

It is not merely that we should be happy, but that we should make others happy, also. This is the true morality.

Immanuel Kant, *Konigsberg Lecture,* 1775

I deny the lawfulness of telling a lie to a sick man, for fear of alarming him. You have no business with the consequences; you are to tell the truth.

Samuel Johnson, in Boswell's *Life,* 1784

Fear is the mother of morality.

Friedrich Nietzsche (1844-1900), in
Beyond Good and Evil, 1886.

Please let me first and always examine myself.

- Synanon Prayer.

Synanon is a San Francisco self-help venture for drug addicts, alcoholics and losers or drop-outs, which succeeds amazingly in psychological rehabilitation through hard physical work, austere living, and closely controlled conference discussions.

Practical Applications of Ethical Theory

Many attempts have been made to develop practical applications of various ethical theories. Usually these reflect the current mores and customs of particular times and places. Thus the Big Boss theory dominated for millenia as social conglomeration occurred. Then the tribal ethic took over until whole cultures, such as in China and India, followed an ethic of harmonious adjustment of oneself and one's environment. All of the vagaries and vicissitudes of European politics were reflected in the ethical theories which rose in their justification. Utilitarianism long served British culture, as pragmatism became applied in the USA business, politics and culture generally.

Many professional groups adopted specific codes of acceptable conduct, as in medicine and law. Usually these codes were applications of unconscious compromises between basic ethical theories, as in medicine where social idealism was compromised, but not harmonized, with hedonism. This occurred also in codes of acceptable legal conduct. Engineering, the military and the clergy, all developed tacit codes of conduct, incorporating various ethical principles in ways designed basically to enhance the dignity and prestige of the professional group concerned.

A continuing difficulty in the practical development of effective standards of ethical practice in any professional organization is the tendency to spell it all out in a codified manner. This legalistic tendency suffers from the same handicap as any code of law: it becomes unwieldy and inconsistent the more it goes into detail. It would be wise for professional organizations to settle on a coherent ethical theory, such as the Aristotelian harmony ethic, and use it as a yardstick for judgment in particular problems that may arise to trouble the organization. Codes of ethics too often are levers for legalism. Too often are they means whereby those in power can control behavior and policy in ways favoring their own interests. Dissenting organization members often can do little except get out, and form their own organization. This they frequently do.

An interesting discussion on literary ethics has been made by the English critic, H. M. Paull (Butterworth, London, 1928, 358 pp.) This is a study in the growth of the literary conscience, and tends to mix up two separate propositions, the moral and the literary conscience. Thus an immoral book may be well written: authors may have high literary consciences, and lamentable morals. But Paull insists, correctly, that standards of morality change with the centuries. Often what were once thought to be innocent practices, gradually come to be regarded as reprehensible, such as polygamy, infanticide, and slavery.

Paull gives many examples of literary crimes and misdemeanors, mostly from English and French literature. Some, however, such as literary thievery or forgery, may be very ancient. As literary crimes, Paull describes not only thievery or forgery, but also piracy of books, abridgements, sequels, and piracy in drama and in sermons. Plagiarism is also discussed as a literary crime. Under literary misdemeanors, Paull includes parodies, hoaxes, and ghost writing. He discusses various ethical problems arising from copyright procedures, anonymous publication and censorship. The ethical standards of editors, reviewers and journalists are explored. Paull goes on to consider the ethical questions arising in connection with various literary forms, such as historical drama and fiction, biography, criticism, and translations. Throughout it is clear that venality plays a large role in literary morality, whether on the part of author or publisher. The story of literary ethics shows clearly that in the long run honesty is the best policy, and that the generous truth will ultimately prevail.

This is the lesson generally to be found in the various attempts to make practical application of ethical theory. It seems to be the case in business, in politics, in professional endeavor, and indeed in ordinary living.

Practical applications of ethical theory in a generalized manner have been carefully considered by that brilliant German philosopher, Leonard Nelson (1882-1927). In his *System of Ethics* (Yale University Press, 1956, 308 pp.), he explores ethical ideas in relation to personality, responsibility, fairness, ideals, and the consequences of beliefs and actions. Based largely on Kant's critiques, he tried the logical analysis of possible methods of establishing workable ethical theories. He himself developed an ethical system, expounded deductively, as by Spinoza. He reaffirmed the common sense of ethical reality, emphasizing the significance of personal dignity in interpersonal relations. He gets around Kant's formalism and moralism by accepting the realities of individual and social conduct at any one time. Thus he compromised Kant's categorical imperatives and optatives with psychological and sociological realities. His ideal is a rational self-determinism.

According to Nelson, a theory of virtues deals with the values of individual conduct, while a theory of right or justice deals with the values of social action. Thus he divides ethics into pure theory and various applications in the following way:

Divisions of Ethics

	Individual Ethics	*Social Ethics*
Pure Ethics	*Theory of Virtue*	*Theory of Right*
Applied Ethics	*Pedagogics*	*Politics*

This is reminiscent of Aristotle's continuation of ethics into the practicalities of politics.

Nelson establishes the logical requirement of an ethical system as the mutual irreducibility of "task" (purpose) and "fact" (verifiable knowledge). In discussing the possibility of a scientific ethic, he asks whether or not ethical problems are soluble in a way similar to that of scientific problems. He points out that Henri Poincaré (1854-1912) had concluded that ethical problems cannot be scientifically settled. Natural science, says Nelson, deals with what does happen (the grammatical indicative), while ethics deals with what ought to happen (the imperative). It can be noted here that what ought to happen can only do so if certain conditions pertinent to the situation are met. What we want to happen (our "ought") can only happen when what we want is possible to happen. Our scientific or verifiable knowledge about ourselves and our environment can help us here; science can tell us, in the light of current verifiability, what is possible. Thus, if we fit our wants to our scientific knowledge, it becomes possible to indicate what ought to happen in a particular situation.

Nelson claims that ethical principles may be valid, even if not observed or followed, but that scientific principles are always both valid and observed in nature. Everyone who wishes to attain a given end is compelled to use the given means, says Nelson, as when anyone desiring to grow a tree must supply it with adequate water to sustain its growth. One might add that our motivation to observe ethical principles depends on our understanding of them, and on our willingness to follow them, or at least to try them out. Their validity is thus tested ("proved") by their observance. And there are many general ethical principles from which one may choose, in order to fit some particular situation.

In his introduction to Nelson's *System of Ethics* Julius Kraft says that contemporary preachments about the discrepancies between the cultivation of science and technology on the one hand and the neglect of ethical theory and practice on the other, often strike a note of insincerity. "All too often these admonitions conceal an appeal to maintain or to return to outworn theological or metaphysical ways. Yet, unless ethics is imbued with the same open-minded approach that is taken for granted in science, the gap between technology and theoretical morality is unlikely to be closed." Kraft goes on to complain that idealism in the pragmatic and utilitarian tradition has been abandoned in favor of a nominalism which defends ethical scepticism. Existentialists tend to promote a pseudo-humanistic authoritarianism, which can go either to anarchy or despotism.

An interesting example of a determined effort to put theoretical principles of ethics into practical application is that attempted by the Institute of Society, Ethics and the Life Sciences, at the Hastings Center, Hastings-on-Hudson, New

York. This is guided by Daniel Callahan and boasts a distinguished advisory group of well known biomedical scientists. Its orientation is predominantly toward the consideration of ethical problems arising from abortion, euthanasia, human experimentation, genetic manipulation, population control, drug abuse, and similar contemporary issues. The Institute publishes monographs on these various topics. These are conventionally prepared, and show little appreciation of the various theories of ethics, which have developed over the centuries. These monographs are thus eclectic in approach, usually with reference to current Judeo-Christian ethical principles.

Nelson's *System of Ethics*, written in the time of anguish between two terrifying world wars, well explores the general aspects of applied ethics. His conclusions seem to be in accord with the rationalistic and scientific approach to ethics as outlined in our discussion so far. Practical applications of theories of ethics will probably be increasingly attempted, not only individually, as people become better acquainted with them, but also socially, in law, in professional organizations, and in matters of public policy.

A Summary of Ethical Theories, with Commentary

There cannot be any one moral rule proposed whereof a person may not justly demand a reason; which would be ridiculous and absurd if it were innate, or so much as self-evident.

> - John Locke (1632-1704), in
>   An Essay Concerning Human
>   Understanding, 1696

The notion of morals implies some sentiment common to all mankind, which recommends the same act to general approbation.

> - David Hume (1711-1776), in
>   An Enquiry Concerning the
>   Principles of Morals, 1751

A moral person is one who is capable of reflecting on past actions and their motives, of approving of some and disapproving of others.

> Charles Darwin (1809-1882), in
> *The Descent of Man*, 1871

In every case I must so act that I can at the same time will that the maxim behind my act should become a universal law.

> Immanuel Kant, *Grundlagen zur Metaphysik der Sitten*, 1785

Summarizing Thus Far

This effort, thus far, has been autobiographical, in the sense that it represents the intellectual progress of one person, myself, now old, in considering that haunting question, *"What am I living for?"* This goes from my earliest notions of motivation and behavior, to please or placate the Big Bosses, my Mother and Father, through my adolescence in compromising my selfish impulses with my altruistic urges, to my maturity in a confusion of often conflicting and disturbing moral formulations, to my old age of acquiescence to what determines my moods and behavior. This individual intellectual journey through ethical theory seems to follow the centuries-long journey of people generally in devising workable formulations as guides to satisfying interpersonal relations. Ontogeny continues to recapitulate phylogeny.

My own ethical position was fairly well formulated by 1945, when I published my essay, "Ethicogenesis" (*Sci. Month.* 60:245-253, 1945). It was derived largely from adaptive survival factors in interpersonal relations, as discussed with Conklin, Herrick, Larsell, Gurchot and Guttentag in 1939 at our seminar session in the Santa Cruz redwoods. We had there tentatively concluded, from the plethora of human experience, that the probability of survival of a relationship between individual people, or groups of people, increases with the extent to which that relationship is mutually satisfying.

It is interesting that this idea was in the air, even as World War II went along. Conrad Hal Waddington, the keen Cambridge biologist, challenged his English colleagues to discuss the relations between science and ethics (*Nature,* 148: 270, 1941). He said that throughout our history our concept of goodness has been considered to require intellectual validity. Four lines of thought have developed, which seem to cast doubt on ethical statements of any claims to rational validation. These are (1) psychoanalytical study, which suggests that our ethical systems are products of our early reactions, sexual or otherwise, to family life; (2) anthropological investigations comparing various social systems, and indicating that ethical beliefs differ extremely from culture to culture, and therefore have no general validity; (3) Marxists' efforts, asserting that ethical systems are expressions of class forces; and (4) the antimetaphysical attempt of logical positivists in studying meaning and developing semantics, and holding that ethical statements have no meaning of a verifiable nature.

However, Waddington felt that these four approaches, far from indicating that science has nothing to do with ethics, show on the contrary that ethical judgments, if based on verifiable facts, may be statements of the same kind as scientific statements. He held that ethics is based on facts of the kind with which scientific effort deals. He said that science may reveal "the nature, the character and direction of the evolutionary process in the world as a whole, and the elucidation of the consequences, in relation to that direction, of various courses of human action." He concluded that "the real good cannot be other than that which has been effective; namely, that which is exemplified in the course of evolution." Waddington held that our moral systems represent ways by which we adapt ourselves to our environment, and thus become able to take part in our own evolutionary progress.

USA scientists also became concerned with ethical problems during World War II. They were on the defensive as a result of the superficial opinion, widely held, that the War and most of our other ills have come upon us as a result of scientific activity. It was, and remains, easy for many people to confuse science, which results in voluntarily agreed upon knowledge we have of ourselves and of our environment, with applications, beneficial or evil, which may be made of this knowledge.

As the debate went on, in England and the USA, it was significant to find three distinguished USA biologists, from three centers of USA culture, agreeing with Waddington (and Julian Huxley) on biological factors which are important in the evolution of ethical ideas. Different considerations led to the same general conclusions on the part of Edwin Grant Conklin (1863-1952) of Princeton, C. Judson Herrick (1868-1969) of Chicago, and Samuel J. Holmes (1886-1964) of California.

Conklin said (*Sci. Month.,* 49:295, 1939), "Biologically life is maintained by continual balance, cooperation, compromise, and the same principles apply to the life of society. The highest level of human development is attained when purpose and freedom, joined to social emotions, training and habits, shape behavior not only for personal but also for social satisfaction. Conduct bringing the broader and more lasting satisfactions is the better."

Herrick remarked (*Sci. Month.,* 40:99, 1940), "That social stability upon which the survival and comfort of individuals depend and that moral satisfaction upon which their equanimity, poise and stability of character depend, arise from the maintenance of relations with their fellows which are mutually advantageous." Holmes stated (*Science,* 90:117, Aug. 11, 1939), "Morality becomes just one phase of the adjustment of people to their conditions of existence. . . . Peoples may believe that their moral customs derive from a supernatural source, but one potent reason for their adoption is their conduciveness to survival."

These opinions are in agreement with those expressed by John Dewey (1858-1952) and his followers as a result of more strictly philosophical studies, to the effect that a moral formulation based on a study of human nature, instead of a disregard for it, would have the facts of humanity continuous with those of the rest of nature, and would thereby ally ethics with physics and biology. Thomas Henry Huxley (1825-1895), a vigorous popularizer of Darwin's view, had tried to expound a similar view, but emphasized the competitive aspect of evolution instead of its adaptive character. His grandson, Julian Sorrel Huxley (1887-   ) expressed himself in a manner similar to Waddington. It might be noted that Dewey's position seems to be an echo of the famed 1847 manifesto of Ludwig, Helmholtz and Du Bois-Reymond that all living phenomena, including consciousness, are explainable in terms of physics and chemistry.

Thomas Huxley in a famed 1893 lecture on *Evolution and Ethics* gave a critical survey of the historical evolution of ethical concepts, and carefully differentiated this from the ethical implications of the theory of natural evolution. Noting that multiplication of people goes on and involves severe competition for the means of support, he says that the strongest, the most self-assertive tend to tread down the weaker. The struggle for existence, he says, tends to eliminate those less fitted to adapt themselves to the conditions of their existence. Evolutionary processes of this sort, however, are checked by social progress, and an ethical process may supervene. The goal of this ethical process, he claims, is not the survival of those who happen to be the fittest, but rather of those who are "ethically the best." By this reasoning he bypasses Nietzsche's power ethic, and means, I suppose, that those people will survive who can adapt themselves to each other. In place of ruthless self-assertion, he calls for self-restraint; instead of thrusting aside competitors, he notes the advantages of cooperation, and instead of the mere survival of the fittest, to influence the fitting of as many as possible to survive. This would be to the advantage of all.

Julian Huxley, writing with humanistic grace and poetical allusion, often expresses a firm rationality about ethics. He calls his ethical position "evolutionary humanism" (*New Bottles for New Wine, Thirteen Essays on Knowledge, Morality, and Destiny,* Harper, New York, 1957; Mentor Books, New York, 1960, 287 pp.). For him, the concept of evolutionary humanism reconciles scientific rationalism with religious aspiration. It gives him an understanding of human nature, always containing possibilities for evil, waste, and destruction, but also for good, for constructive welfare, and for individual and social happiness. For him, as for Conklin, there is a cultural evolution as well as a biological one, and the capacity for adaptiveness is a deciding factor in survival, whether culturally or biologically.

The survival aspect of evolution seems to be equally important in biology and culture. There is a better chance for continuing existence for that individual person or group which adjusts harmoniously toward other individuals or groups than for those which do not. In adjustments of individuals or groups of people in harmonious conduct toward each other there seems to be a greater tendency toward mutual satisfaction and mutual benefit than when such adjustment does not exist. As put by Ray Lepley (*Verifiability of Value,* Columbia University Press, New York, 1944, 280 pp.), "The forces of life and existence afford constant and recurring dynamic for attempts to make satisfactory adjustments. In these attempts, intelligence and reason are increasingly needed. They are and will be effective, so far as they can be, in the degree that they operate as elements within an inclusive experimental procedure." Adaption toward a goal of mutual satisfaction might become an ethical basis for effective "biological engineering."

The technology of genetic manipulation, however, raises serious ethical problems, as foreseen in Aldous Huxley's *Brave New World* (New York, 1932). In this famed novel, Aldous Huxley warns of moral anarchy in abuse of technology, by depicting a repulsive Utopia, in which a Platonic harmony is achieved by genetic manipulation and continuing psychological conditioning, with a society of human robots, for whom happiness is merely unconscious subordination.

Conklin emphasized the importance of promoting harmonious adaptation. "In all normal human beings it is possible to cultivate unselfishness, sympathy rather than enmity, cooperation rather than antagonism. Human nature can be improved by human nurture." All of education, over the centuries, has been predicated upon this premise. It operates, as one generally knows from one's mother's breast, on hope of reward and fear of punishment.

If our scientific knowledge of ourselves and of our environment does have ethical consequences, as many of us believe, it should be possible to discover an operative natural principle relating to human conduct which can be stated in descriptive terms. We should be able to *carefully* observe factors operating in human conduct as to then describe them accurately without the intrusion into our observation of the emotions of fear or hope. It may be asking a lot to try to reach this ideal, but it is part of the scientific progress.

There seems to be little to be gained by exhorting people to be good. This has been the way of moralists for centuries, and it hasn't worked very well. Neither fear of punishment nor hope of reward has been fully successful in promoting good conduct among people. There has hardly been knowledge enough among us to reach agreement, as Locke would have hoped, as to what constitutes the "good," or as to what is "right."

For ages philosophers have wrestled with the problem of human conduct from the standpoint of absolute criteria for "goodness." We now realize that there are no absolutes, except as asymptotically receding ideals. Our verifiable knowledge about ourselves and our environment continually grows, and thus is subject to modification and revision. Thus even as "truth" is now recognized as being relative to our increasing precision in scientific search for it, so also does it seem that our concepts of "goodness" and "right" are relative, tentative only, and subject to revision as our verifiable knowledge of ourselves increases.

In general, in the light of our current scientific knowledge, some of us may agree that it is "good" for any individual or group of individuals as such to survive. Some may doubt this. The doubters might hold that under certain trying conditions self-sacrifice is "good," at least for those outsiders who may be inspired to worthiness by such self-sacrifice. However, the ones who sacrifice themselves are gone, and have no more capacity themselves to participate in any "good." They and their acts survive in the memories of those inspired by them. This may contribute to the general social "good," and it remains a survival.

Individuals and groups of individuals are usually in some kind of relationship with other individuals or groups. Do such relationships have survival value? Is this survival value of significance in social evolution? There seems to be scientific agreement that the process of evolution is continuing. With living things it turns out that most mutations of genes, whether caused by radiation or otherwise, result in death. Those mutants which survive do so as a consequence of adaptation even though the potential for lethal mutation continues. Among us humans there are many who carry "inborn errors" of metabolic processes, which are genetically transmissible. By selective breeding we may be able to weed out deleterious genes. Since it appears that many psychological aspects of our lives are associated with metabolic processes, it is reasonable to assume that we can actually, if we wish, and if we are patient enough, breed out undesirable psychological traits, such as greed, arrogance, aggressiveness, cruelty, and intolerance, and breed in the tendencies toward generosity, goodwill, kindliness, and relaxed tolerance.

Of course, environmental factors play a role in shaping our individual tendencies toward either individual or social "goodness" or "badness." This is the conditioning process to which all of us are subject. Yet it may well be that within each of us there are the genetically determined metabolic processes that point us in one direction or the other. It is this problem, with its ethical relation to racism, that is being debated currently at Stanford University by two of its opinionated Nobelates, William Bradford Shockley (1910-   ), Professor of Physics, who opts for genetic determinism, and Joshua Lederberg (1925-   ), Professor of Genetics, who favors environment as a major factor in personality. Shockley recommends study of eugenic breeding, in an effort to eliminate dysgenic genes. This is a current echo of the ideas of Francis Galton (1822-1911), a cousin of Charles Darwin. Shockley's views have now been contested in a court action brought by a Nigerian student.

Many current ethical problems seem to be associated with the "new permissiveness." This is a phenomenon of irregular cyclical occurrence, and it is usually associated with the ups and downs of Americo-European sex mores. Times of strong puritanical repression of overt sexual activity and expression are followed after a few generations with a period of apparent licentiousness, looseness of talk, and relaxation of social or police control. With current rapid and worldwide communication, the "new permissiveness' spreads even to such traditionally strict peoples as the Japanese. Yet, the basic ethical problems remain: the general social condemnation of individuals who, for their own gain, exploit or profit from the ignorance, poverty, cupidity, or the hunger and sex drives of others. Involved then are the ancient "vices" of gambling, prostitution, drunkenness, drug addiction, and vagrancy.

When these "vices" are socially repressed, corruption of

police and public officials inevitably follows, as well as
blackmail and exploitation of those caught in the "vices."
Gambling seems to be a universal lure among all peoples and
at all times. Dishonesty in gambling seems also to be a part of
the "action" everywhere and whenever. Loaded dice have been
found in the ruins of Pompeii, and card-sharks have flourished
since playing cards first appeared. A fair summary of current
gambling conditions in the USA is given in a staff survey
appearing in *Newsweek* for April 10, 1972, pp. 46-52.

Gambling seems to flourish under the influence of such
universal psychological factors as greed, hope, and daring.
Full knowledge of the odds placed against the gambler seems
to be only a slight deterrant to those craving the excitement of
the play in the hope of a win at the next chance. This attitude
extends to "playing the stockmarket," and to all sorts of
business, commercial and industrial ventures in which risk is
present. This has "paid-off" as long as we hold to the notion of
an "endless frontier" or to "inexhaustible natural resources."
When they're used up, what then? Some of us seem now to be
realizing that continual growth, whether of population, or
capital, may be dangerous to the future welfare of our species.
We are those who are willing to sacrifice some of our
immediate individual welfare for the future welfare of our
descendants. We also tend to consider the future consequences
of our present activities. Others of us do not, and furthermore,
even in knowledge of what may happen, do not care. The basic
ethical choices, of which we have been aware since antiquity,
are still with us.

Whether in gambling, prostitution, drunkenness, drug addiction, or vagrancy, the ones involved who seem generally to
incur the opprobium of society are those who exploit and
profit from the rackets associated with their exploitation, the
pimps, procurers, touts, fixers, bookies, dealers, bagmen,
pushers, bootleggers and panderers. However, as the profits
mount, other bullying entrepreneurs band together to wrest
control of the loot. The USA experiment to prohibit alcoholic
beverages spawned organized racketeering and corruption,
and led to murder, extortion, and villainy in general. This was

continued by the "mobs," generally Sicilian, known collec-
tively as the Mafia. Usually those in control masqueraded
under extreme hypocritical respectability with flashy clothes,
automobiles, gems, and mistresses, and elaborate public
funerals for their slain. Venal lawyers kept those at the top
from legal social sanction, and corruption of police, and of
public officials, was a well-recognized part of the picture.
Furthermore, otherwise respectable banking concerns often
were found to be the owners of whorehouses and gambling
salons. Thus had it been in Imperial Rome.

Physicians are usually well aware of these practical moral
problems. Thus, William Dock, long a witty and wise professor of medicine, makes the pertinent observation (*New Eng.
Journ. Med.,* Nov. 2, 1972, as quoted by "Fearless Spectator,
Charles McCabe):

> "In New York, gambling has been made legal and is
> heavily taxed; also it is widely advertised, even in the
> subways. Why not the same thing for alcohol, marijuana,
> heroin, cocaine and guns?
>
> "If the tax is just high enough not to make evasion
> profitable, it ends 'pushing' by profiteers .... Two herbal
> products have passed into world-wide use since their
> discovery. These are tobacco, which calms without sedat-
> ing, and hops, a close cousin of marijuana .... In the 19th
> Century fluid extracts of marijuana and hops were in the
> U. S. Formulary .... recommended as 'tonics' and 'sopo-
> rifics'. They were the best tranquilizers."

While the free use of alcoholic beverages, heroin, morphine,
hemp, cocaine, and similar restricted drugs has a potentiality
of harm both for individual users and their societies, this might
be much less than the harm resulting from their prohibition.
The principle of *laissez faire* might well apply. It would surely
reduce our ever-burdensome bureaucracy.

A recent significant ethical problem attracting much public
concern is what is called "conflict of interest." It is open to
question that a judge, for example, would really be fair in
sitting on a corporation case, in which he was a director of the
corporation. This situation concerns the general social prob-

lem of bribery, undertaken to curry favor. Bribery poses many difficult ethical problems, in spite of the fact that it is generally condemned. It is rather common, however, in various disguised ways, in business or political transactions. One would expect that the management of great corporations, which exist ostensibly for promoting social welfare, would be scrupulous about avoiding the slightest suspicion of bribery. Unfortunately, this is not the case. However, public confidence in corporations is promptly reflected in the stockmarket. International Telephone and Telegraph, ITT, for example, has learned the painful way that honesty, after all, is the best policy, and that any public suspicion of trying to influence political decisions with money is apt to force some degree of rectitude.

Bribery figures heavily in spying, counter-spying, and "intelligence." An intelligent person might reasonably doubt that only good is served by this elaborate apparatus and expense. With the wide and rapid distribution of scientific information, it is to be expected that intelligent people anywhere will make what applications of such knowledge they can make. Even the basic technological principles are now well known, including applications to warfare or to economic behavior. Pertinent to this is the important study, *Theory of Games and Economic Behavior* (Princeton University Press, 1944, 320 pp.), by the great computer pioneer, John Von Neuman (1903-1957). In this it is demonstrated that in the long run in an adversary intellectual game, such as two-handed, straight poker, one will tend to come out ahead if one goes on the premise that one's opponent knows every card in one's hand. Consider chess, where every potentiality is before both players. It is the psychology of concealment and deception that takes too much of one's attention.

The bribery associated with spying is often too great to resist in some people in places of trust, or with some misguided discontents, and sex often plays a part, as innumerable suspense novels of the James Bond type suggest. Too often this situation results in anguish and shame. Traitors to a trust are usually scorned by everyone, including those who have bribed them. So it is with police informers. There has always been disdain for tattle-tales, squealers, or finks. Even children dislike those who betray a confidence. This is recognition of the moral obligation to justify a trust.

In writing on *"The Ideals of Science in Relation to National Security"* (*Texas Rep. Biol. Med.,* 13: 434-445, 1955), during our miserable time with McCarthyism, I said, "The authoritarian methods by which our security regulations are enforced, are detrimental to our best scientific interests, and indeed to our very safety." I went on to say that, in addition to giving a false sense of strength and safety, "our security procedures inhibit the very work of our scientists and technologists on which our safety and welfare depend." Agreeing with what George Sarton said previously, I stated, "It is the duty of those who are concerned with the philosophical significance of science to continue steadfastly to tell the people what science is about, and what the standards of scientists are. This is something beyond the usual sort of popularization of science. It calls for much patience and tact. If it can succeed in reducing the threat of authoritarian control of American scientists, it will be worth everything that it may take."

Conflict of interest covers a wide range of human behavior from flagrant bribery of public officials, through spying of all kinds, to family squabbles in which parents are often both accusers and judges. This latter situation is frequently met in various hierarchial conditions, even when appeal to a higher authority is possible. Conflict of interest may include many subtle instances of bribery by threat or promise, or by flattery or frowning. Conflict of interest enters into many business and legal situations. M. W. Childs and D. Cater have given a perceptive survey of some of these problems in *Ethics in a Business Society* (Mentor Books, New York, 1954, 184 pp.). This problem of conflict of interest is a major matter in the new code of deportment for lawyers and judges, as recommended to the American Bar Association.

Basically, conflict of interest involves some aspect of dishonesty, not only with others but also with oneself. Whenever one suspects that one may be getting tangled in it, one would be wise to get out. When one in any position of responsibility and authority loses the confidence of those who are related to it, resignation from it seems to be the proper and dignified action to take. In a working democracy, this seems to be expected.

Conflict of interest enters many ordinary situations. An ancient aspect of it is nepotism, when someone in authority appoints, or arranges the appointment of, (often by bribery), some relative or relatives to lucrative positions in the organization. In political situations this is often an accepted fact of life, especially in dictatorships or authoritarian governments. It can be scandalous, as with the Borgias in the Church, or it may be benign, as when a family controls a business. Yet, ethically a conflict usually remains between the hedonistic motivations of the ones involved in the nepotism, on the one hand, and the usual socially idealistic motivation professed by the organization, on the other hand. The general social response to the degree of responsibility and integrity shown by those involved is often the deciding factor. When there is any doubt, it would seem the part of wisdom in acknowledging the responsibility to resign with dignity from the position which might give offense. This is a worthy aspect of governmental responsibility whenever a question of conflict of interest arises.

In his keen and perceptive essay on "Ethical Problems of Medical Reserach" (*Mainstreams of Medicine,* University of Texas Press, Austin, 1971, pp. 152-180), Henry Knowles Beecher (1904-   ), Dorr Professor of Anesthesia at Harvard, raises the ethical-legal issue of "invasion of privacy." This concept arose as a result of a brilliant essay by a couple of Harvard law students, S. D. Warren and Louis D. Brandeis (1856-1941) on "The Right to Privacy" (*Harvard Law Rev.,* 4:193-220, 1890). They noted that "political, social and economic changes entail the recognition of new rights, and the common law, in its eternal youth, grows to meet the demands of society. . . . .There came recognition of our spiritual nature, of our feelings, and our intellect. Gradually the scope of legal rights broadened; and now the right to life has come to mean the right to enjoy life, "the right to be let alone." "Rights" thus become legal expressions of ethical standards.

Beecher restricts his discussion to the invasion of privacy which may occur in any kind of human experimentation. The principle, however, now widely accepted legally, extends to many kinds of police spying, wiretapping, bugging, search without warrant, or even "protective arrest." Human experimentation generally involves many problems, as Beecher shows. Usually, it is oriented toward acquiring biochemical, physiological, psychological, or sociological information. It is an essential part of the testing of new drugs. My own experience and ethical reflection thereon is summarized in an address on "Ethical Theories and Human Experimentation" (*Annals N. Y. Acad. Sci.,* 169: 388-395, 1970). There is quite a flood of writing on the subject.

The experimenters are biased pragmatically, and justify their human experimentation more on the basis of promoting social welfare than of furthering the welfare of the experimental subject. When the "subject" is a patient, however, in a clinic or hospital, justification can be made on the basis of treatment, or even diagnosis or prevention of disease, and thus for the patient's welfare. Actually every medical handling of a patient, for diagnosis, prevention or treatment of disease, or for maintenance of health, is an experiment, in the sense that the outcome is not precisely predictable. This thus seems to be another example of what René Dubos calls "statistical morality."

A major moral problem for the medical profession, as for every other organized group, remains from antiquity: to choose action on the basis of welfare of an individual, or of welfare of the group, or of humanity as a whole, or indeed of our world itself. Currently the dignity and worthiness of each individual is being stressed, largely as a backlash from the dehumanization resulting from the application of our scientific knowledge and technology in machines, computers, and corporate and government industry. The problem remains of achieving a harmonious balance between the welfare of individuals and the welfare of our species and of our world. This calls for much responsibility on individuals to adjust themselves to others and to their environment, so that all may happily survive.

With so many more people in the world than ever before, however, tensions are often unbearable, especially in large cities, and violence is often endemic. The psychodynamism of frustration too often goes to blind rage, and innocent people often become victims of cruel beatings and murder. Serious crime is commonplace now in the USA. What to do? As an editorial in the *Wall Street Journal* (April 11, 1972) suggests, in commenting on Sydney Hook's proposal that we seek compassionate understanding, we would be wise to regard the problems of victims of crimes with the same solicitude as we regard the human and civil rights of criminals and of those accused of crime.

One might think that our current moralizing about law and order would have some practical popular effect. This does not seem ever to be the case. The ethical theories so vigorously debated by some of our intellectuals seem seldom to reach the street or the marketplace. People always seem to be aware of the general trend of current laws, but also to be anxious to evade them when it is to their advantage to do so. In times of high culture, as in the Renaissance, or of intellectual enlightenments, as in 19th Century Europe and England, misery, squalor, and crime was rife in ghettoes and slums, while powerful and flashing leaders were often little more than the most callous criminals, as with Cesare Borgia (1476-1507), or Maxmillian Robespierre (1758-1794). So it continues, with Hitlers, Mussolinis or Stalins, or in the USA, with the Mafia "Godfathers."

Often the Sicilian Mafia "families" display a high standard of in-group rectitude and honor. Yet, they prey callously on the ghetto and slum inhabitants of the big cities in which they flourish, and they are coldly murderous among themselves, for control of the huge profits from their racketeering with drugs, gambling and prostitution. This is what prohibitions spawn. Among themselves, the Mafia are "good"; to the social order they are poison.

This mixture of good and evil is often characteristic, it seems, of those who seek great power, as seen historically in such figures as Alexander the Great, Genghis Khan, Tamerlane, Henry VIII, Peter the Great, Mussolini, and Hitler.

An extraordinary example of how an amazing mixture of

calculated good and deliberate evil can be used to obtain power, is told by Helen Holdredge in her account of San Francisco's Voodoo Queen, *"Mammy Pleasant"* (Portuan, New York, 1953, 312 pp.). This seems merely to be a recent expression of Machiavelli.

With all the complexities of our current scene, it seems more clear than ever that there is validity to the proposed naturally operating principle, that the probability of survival of relationships between individuals or groups of individuals increases with the extent to which these relationships are mutually satisfying. But oh! there is so much more to say!

Concluding Note

Nothing is more certain in this uncertain world than that there is no final or universal answer to that complex question of *"What are we living for?"* Our moods change, and with them, our purposes, and we are so different from each other. Yet we are steadily learning more, in a verifiable way, about ourselves and the world around us. Thus our answers to the question of what we are living for increase in validity as our knowledge of ourselves grows.

As a tentative approach to a generalization on what we are living for, the evidence suggests that it is: to be satisfied. Our biological set-up is such that for self-preservation we become satisfied with food, and for species preservation with sexual activity resulting in orgasm. As for our interpersonal relations, it seems that they are governed, however loosely, by the general principle that the probability of survival of a relationship between individuals or groups of individuals increases with the extent to which the relationship is mutually satisfying. The conditionable mid-brain, gut-feeling, biologically-set sense of satisfaction do seem to be paramount in ethics, at least as of now.

INDEX OF PERSONAL NAMES

178

Kipling, R. (1865-1936), 7
Knox, John (1505-1572), 75
Kraft, Julius, 156
Kraft-Ebing, Richard (1840-1902), 123
Kropotkin, Peter (1842-1921), 31
Kurtz, Paul, 134

Lamarck, Chevalier (J. B. P de Monet) (1744-1829), 96
Lamont, Corliss, 134
Lao-Tzu, 22, 44
Larsell, Olaf (1886-1966), 10, 139
Lawrence, David Herbert (1885-1930), 121
Lederberg, Joshua (1925-), 165
Leibniz, Gottfried Wilhelm (1646-1716), 83
Lenin, Vladimir Ilyich (1870-1924), 129
Lepley, Ray, 163
Leonardo da Vinci (1452-1519), 71
LeVey, Anton Szandor, 77
Levey, Martin, 51
Locke, John (1632-1704), 84, 158
Loevenhart, Arthur (1878-1929), 8
Loyola, Ignatius (1491-1556), 80
Lucretius (99-55 BC), 41
Ludwig, Karl Friedrich Wilhelm (1816-1895), 139
Luther, Martin (1483-1536), 74
Lysenko, Trofim Denisovich (1898-), 96

Machiavelli, Nicolo (1469-1527), 73
MacLean, Paul D., 143
MacLeish, Archibald, 28

MacPherson, P. B., 81
Mallarme, Stephane (1842-1898), 124
Malthus, Thomas Robert (1766-1834), 100
Maimonides, Moses (1135-1204), 69
Marshall, George, 113
Marcus Aurelius Antoninus (121-180), 52
Marcuse, Herbert (1898-), 131
Marx, Karl (1818-1883), 129, 139
Maslow, Abraham (1908-1971), 118
Masters, William Howell (1915-), 122
McCabe, Charles, 65, 120
McKeown, Raymond, 9
Mead, Margaret (1901-), 126
Meek, Walter (1878-1963), 8
Mencius (4th Cent. BC), 45
Merezhkowski, Dimitri (1865-1941), 60, 72
Methuselah, 32
Michelangelo (1475-1564), 72
Mill, James (1773-1836), 93
Mill, John Stuart (1806-1873), 95
Miller, William Snow (1858-1939), 8, 9
Mohammed (570-632), 56
Montagu, Ashley, 32
Montagu, William Pepperell (1873-1953), 142
Montaigne, Michel (1533-1592), 78
Moore, George Edward (1873-1958), 55, 109

Nelson, Leonard (1882-1927), 154
Neuman, John von (1903-1957), 168

SUBJECT INDEX

Sex drive, chemical factors in, 145
Sex ethic, 58, 119
Sex-oriented "Sin", 58
Sexual activity and evil, 33, 58, 76, 119
Sin, concept of, 30, 39, 65
Sin, sex-oriented, 58
Sins, the seven deadly, 46, 63
Situational ethic, the, 136
Slavery, 54, 90, 111
Snakes, 60
Social Health, 133
Social idealism, ethic of, 37, 39, 41
Social satisfaction, 99
Social stability, 161
Soviet system, 129
Stoicism, ethics of, 52
Strength of sin in the law, 59
Survival of the fittest, 97, 135, 162
Syphilis, 76
Systems dynamics, 135

Taoism, 45
Technology, problems of, 90, 114, 135
Texas Reports on Biology and Medicine, 86
Thirteenth, "Greatest of Centuries", 69
Totemism, 39

Trade, influence of, 70
Tribal ethic, 35, 153
Trinitarians, 56
Trivium, 64
Truth, 16, 72
Tyranny, 73

Unitarian, 56
Universal reason, 68
Universals, 68
Utilitarianism, 92, 94, 153

Venality, 74, 167
Vice, 120
Victimless laws, 120
Violence, 129, 131
Virtue, 49, 92
Virtues, the four cardinal, 63

Way of life of Lao-Tzu, The, 44
Wickedness, 62
Witchcraft, 77
Work-ethic, 90

Yoga, 46
Youth, revolt of, 4, 81, 128

Zoroastrian dichotomy of goodness and evil, 30